# Piano, the Instrument

*An Annotated Bibliography*

Michiko Ishiyama Wolcott

The Scarecrow Press, Inc.
Lanham, Maryland, and London
2001

# SCARECROW PRESS, INC.

Published in the United States of America
by Scarecrow Press, Inc.
4720 Boston Way, Lanham, Maryland 20706
www.scarecrowpress.com

4 Pleydell Gardens, Folkestone
Kent CT20 2DN, England

British Library Cataloguing-in-Publication Information Available

**Library of Congress Cataloging-in-Publication Data**

Wolcott, Michiko Ishiyama, 1969–
    Piano, the instrument : an annotated bibliography / Michiko Ishiyama Wolcott.
      p. cm.
    Includes indexes.
    ISBN 0-8108-4052-9 (alk. paper)
     1. Piano—Bibliography. I. Title.
    ML128.P3 W65 2001
    016.7862'19—dc21                   2001020728

# Contents

# Contents

# Preface

This is an annotated bibliography about the piano itself. Although there is much information easily attainable relating to piano literature, performance, and pedagogy, a comprehensive bibliography that gathered information about the piano itself had not existed, save for a few very selective bibliographies.

The materials included are limited to writings in English published before 2000. *Piano, the Instrument: An Annotated Bibliography* includes such topics as the history and development of the piano, its construction, and maintenance/repair. The treatise does not address tone production or temperament. Editorials, letters, replies, reviews, and business and legal documents are not included. Furthermore, catalogs and advertising flyers from manufacturers and dealers are excluded, since similar information is available in other publications. Information about other keyboard instruments such as the harpsichord, combination instruments such as the piano-organ, and the digital, electronic, player, reproducing, or other mechanical pianos are included only if it is directly relevant to the piano. Every item included in the bibliography has been examined firsthand.

The bibliography is organized into six sections by topic: general information, history, builders and manufacturers, construction and design, maintenance and repair, and miscellaneous subjects. The first section lists works containing general information, including but not limited to books and articles covering a wide range of topics, introductory materials, and serial titles. The second section covers the history of the piano and is arranged by country. The section on piano builders and manufacturers is arranged by the name of builder or manufacturer. The sections on construction and maintenance are arranged by parts of the piano. The section on miscellaneous subjects includes catalogs for collections of instruments, works about pedal pianos, pianos associated with composers, selection and purchase, works intended for younger readers, and works about other miscellaneous topics not included above. Entries addressing multiple topics are cross-referenced by shortening the second and subsequent appearances of the work as follows:

> Fine, Larry. *The Piano Book: Buying & Owning a New or Used Piano. See 408 under* Construction and Design—General Construction.

Readers are referred to the subject index for further cross-referencing.

I am grateful to the following people: James Streem, for his direction and guidance; Anne Garee, for her continuous encouragement and support; Rita Warwick, who provided editorial assistance; Shawn Wolcott, Wen Wing, and countless others who made this book a reality.

# General

1.  Allen, Robert Thomas. "A Piano Is Polite, Genteel. It Gives Your Home Class. And If You Can Play It, So Much the Better." *Ragtimer* (May–June 1978): 15–20.

    Originally published in *The Toronto Star*, October 14, 1972. An introductory article about the piano. Addresses history, construction, industry, literature, and performance. Includes anecdotes involving a piano. Also mentions player pianos.

2.  Baines, Anthony. *The Oxford Companion to Musical Instruments*. Oxford: Oxford University Press, 1992.

    "Piano" (pp. 254–63). Addresses construction, history, and literature. Photographs, labeled illustrations of the actions. Also see "Fortepiano," p. 120. The appendix is an alphabetical list of makers of musical instruments. Bibliography.

3.  Ballantine, Bill. *The Piano: An Introduction to the Instrument*. Keynote Books. New York: Franklin Watts, 1971.

    A general information book about the piano, primarily intended for beginners. Topics include construction, history, builders and manufacturers, performance and performers, composers and literature, and basic maintenance of the instrument. Photographs, illustrations (many labeled). Glossary, selective bibliography, and selective discography. 128 pp.

4.  Briggs, G[ilbert] A[rthur]. *Pianos, Pianists, and Sonics*. 1st ed. New York: Herman & Stephens, 1951.

Topics include history, construction, types of piano, piano tone, piano touch, acoustics, selecting a piano, care and maintenance, recording, pedagogy, accompanying, and performers. Photographs, illustrations. Glossary. 192 pp.

5.    Burton, Ken. *"Dear Dr. Piano . . . ": Piano Facts and Fun.* Calgary, Alberta: Dot Press, 1993.

Illustrated by Ben Crane. A general information book in a question-and-answer format. Topics include purchase, construction, tuning, maintenance and care, climate, and working with a piano tuner. Some information (such as climate and price quotes) is particular to the Calgary, Alberta, area at the time of publication. Intended for beginners and young piano students. 203 pp.

6.    Dearling, Robert, ed. *The Illustrated Encyclopedia of Musical Instruments.* New York: Schirmer Books, 1996.

Includes a section on the piano. Addresses the history of the piano, early French, English, and Viennese pianos, the modern piano, and the modern concert grand. A list of piano types and their definitions. Photographs, illustrations. 240 pp.

7.    Everett Piano Company. *The Art and Science of Buying a Piano.* Buena Park, Calif.: Everett Piano Company, 1983.

An introductory guide to the history, construction, maintenance, and purchase of the piano. Glossary of some technical terms. This is not a catalog of Everett instruments, and the company is not specifically named in the text (other than in illustrations); however, it is probably intended for promotional purposes. Illustrations. 16 pp.

8.    Gaines, James R., ed. *The Lives of the Piano.* New York: Holt, Rinehart and Winston, 1981.

A collection of articles concerning various topics about the piano such as history, literature, people, and the musical environment. The relevant articles are: 1. "The Well-Tempered Revolution: A Consideration of the Piano's Social and Intellectual History," by Anthony Burgess; 2. "Enlightenment's Gift to the Age of

Romance: How the Piano Came to Be," by Annalyn Swan; and 3. "Of Wood and Iron Wrought: The Making of a Bösendorfer," by Anthony Riversidge. Photographs, illustrations. Biographies of the Authors. 215 pp.

9.   Gill, Dominic, ed. *The Book of the Piano.* Ithaca, N.Y.: Cornell University Press, 1981.

A collection of articles on various topics about the piano. Of the articles, the following are relevant: "Prologue," an overview of the history of the instrument, by Dominic Gill; "The Anatomy of the Piano," addressing the construction of the piano, by Derek Adlam; "The American Piano," addressing piano building and manufacturing in America, by William Brooks; "The Piano Makers," addressing the history of builders and manufacturers, by Andrew Clemens; and "Eccentric Pianos," addressing unusual pianos, by Andrew Clemens. Photographs, illustrations. Glossary, bibliography, discography. 288 pp.

10.   Greenfield, Jack. "Sound Background: Acoustics of Piano, a Bibliography." *Piano Technicians Journal* 28, no. 3 (March 1985): 23–26.

An unannotated bibliography by Thomas D. Rossing. Prepared for a class at the Northern Illinois Piano Technicians Seminar in DeKalb, Ill. in 1984. Includes books, papers, articles, and theses. Also includes a partial list of books and papers on scales, tuning, and temperament.

11.   Hester, Richard. *Introduction to the Fortepiano: In 20 Questions More or Less.* The Early Piano. Coeymans Hollow, N.Y.: Richard Hester Pianos, 1987.

Topics include design and construction, restoration, maintenance and tuning, sound and acoustics, evaluation, technique, and performance. Illustrations (some labeled, some accompanied by detailed tables). A list of recent magazine articles and a list of related organizations and publications. 33 pp.

12.   Hinson, Maurice. *Keyboard Bibliography.* Cincinnati: Music

Teachers National Association, 1968.

A selective unannotated bibliography on keyboard pedagogy, construction and design, performance, and literature. Includes books on organs, harpsichords, clavichords, and pianos. The section on construction and design contains sixteen items. 18 pp.

13. ———. *The Pianist's Bookshelf: A Practical Guide to Books, Videos, and Other Resources.* Bloomington: Indiana University Press, 1998.

A selective annotated bibliography of books, theses, dissertations, and videos published after 1987 and currently (as of 1988) in print. The entries are arranged alphabetically regardless of subject; a subject index follows the bibliography. Topics include performance, aesthetics, biographies, construction, editors, performers, teachers, writers, history, literature, pedagogy, and technique. The construction and design index lists twenty-seven entries, some of which are cross-classified. The appendix is an alphabetical list of publishers mentioned in the bibliography, with their mailing addresses. 323 pp.

14. ———. *The Pianist's Reference Guide: A Bibliographical Survey.* Los Angeles: Alfred Publishing Co., 1987.

A selective annotated bibliography of books, dissertations, and theses related to the piano. Entries are alphabetically ordered regardless of subject, and users are referred to the subject index for more specific searches. Topics covered are related primarily to literature, performance, and pedagogy; however, there is a limited number of works on piano construction. The appendix lists publishers that appear in the bibliography. 336 pp.

15. ———. *The Piano Teacher's Source Book: An Annotated Bibliography of Books Related to the Piano and Piano Music.* With a preface by William S. Newman. 2nd ed. Melville, N.Y.: Belwin Mills, 1980.

Contains information about selected books and dissertations on performance, composers and literature, pedagogy, history, and construction and design. Includes items on harpsichords and clavichords. Some entries are not annotated. Author index, composer index, and a list of publishers. 187 pp.

16. Kentner, Louis. *Piano*. Yehudi Menuhin Music Guides. New York: Schirmer Books, 1976.

An introductory book on piano history, construction, technique, and literature. Part 1 is dedicated to the history and construction of the instrument. Photographs, illustrations. Bibliography, discography. 210 pp.

17. Kresge, Don U., comp. *What Your Piano Is All About and Allied Subjects*. Durham, N.C.: by the compiler, 1974.

A compilation of articles written by Maurice Krakauer Bretzfelder, C. W. Anderson, Kawai Piano American Corporation, Steinway & Sons, and Story & Clark Company. Topics include history, construction, manufacturing, acoustics, tuning, and maintenance and care. Includes a section on frequently asked questions about basic care and maintenance. Photographs, illustrations. 147 pp.

18. May, Katharine. "Instruments: The Fortepiano." *Early Music Today* 4, no. 5 (October–November 1996): 14–17.

Addresses the history, purchase, restoration, and performers of the fortepiano. Includes a list of museums and private collections and a list of builders and restorers. Photograph. Bibliography, discography.

19. *The New Encyclopaedia Britannica*. 15th ed. 32 vols. Chicago: Encyclopaedia Britannica, 1998. S.v., "Musical Instruments."

In vol. 24, pp. 651–706. By Sir Jack Allan Westrup and others. Includes a section on stringed keyboard instruments (by Edwin M. Ripin and Laurence Elliot Libin) that discusses clavichord, harpsichord, piano, organ, and other related keyboard instruments. Topics include construction, history, tuning and temperament, among others. Illustrations (labeled). Bibliography at the end of the article. Also see "Piano" (vol. 9, p. 417), "Square Piano" (vol. 11, p. 185), and other related entries.

20.  Oringer, Judith. *Passion for the Piano*. With a foreword by André
     Watts. Los Angeles: Jeremy P. Tarcher, 1983.

     While this is a general information book for beginning pian-
     ists, it discusses the history of the piano, manufacturing, selecting
     and purchasing, and general maintenance. Also includes a chapter
     on references to piano in literature, film, and politics. Photo-
     graphs, illustrations. Glossary, bibliography ("Recommended
     Reading"). 167 pp.

21.  Palmer, King. *The Piano*. 3rd ed. Teach Yourself Books. Seven-
     oaks, England: Hodder and Stoughton, 1986. Reprint, Lincoln-
     wood, Ill.: NTC Publishing Group, 1992.

     A general information book for beginners. Includes a short
     section on the construction, selection, and basic maintenance of
     the piano. Illustrations. 151 pp.

22.  Palmieri, Robert, ed. *Encyclopedia of Keyboard Instruments*,
     vol. 1, *The Piano*. New York: Garland Publishing, 1994.

     Discusses primarily topics related to the construction and
     development of the piano, such as important builders and manu-
     facturers, composers who influenced the development of the
     piano, construction, and miscellaneous subjects. An entry may
     contain a definition, background information about the topic,
     photographs and/or illustrations, and a bibliography. Many entries
     are signed. A list of contributors at the end of the book. 521 pp.

23.  ———. *Piano Information Guide: An Aid to Research*. Music
     Research and Information Guides, no. 10. Garland Reference Li-
     brary of the Humanities, no. 806. New York: Garland Publishing,
     1989.

     A selective annotated bibliography of books, theses, disserta-
     tions, and articles about the piano. In two parts: part 1, "The In-
     strument," and part 2, "The Music." Topics covered in part 1 (282
     entries) include automated pianos, electronic pianos, tuning and
     temperament, general construction, maintenance and care, and
     history of the instrument. Appendix A: a chronology of important
     events in the development of the piano; appendix B: a list of piano

categories in five languages (English, German, French, Italian, and Spanish). Subject and author-title indices. Photographs, illustrations. 329 pp.

24. *Piano Technicians Journal.* Kansas City, Mo.: Piano Technicians Guild.

Serial (monthly), from January 1958. Combines the former *Tuners' Journal* and the *Piano Technician*. Topics include history of the instrument, construction and design, repair, restoration, maintenance and care, tuning, temperament, training of piano technicians, and history of piano technology. Includes reprints of articles published in other journals and magazines.

25. Preisman, Albert. "The Piano." *Audio Engineering* 37, no. 10 (October 1953): 26–30, 111–14; no. 11 (November 1953): 22–24, 64–69.

Discusses the history, construction, and acoustics of the piano. Photographs, illustrations (labeled). Bibliography.

26. Randel, Don, ed. *The New Harvard Dictionary of Music.* Cambridge, Mass.: Harvard University Press, Belknap Press, 1986.

See "Piano" (pp. 629–36) by Charles P. Fisher. Bibliography by Christopher C. Hill. A brief overview of the history of the instrument. Illustrations include those of various actions in detail, extensively labeled. Also see under other relevant terms.

27. Ripin, Edwin M., Cyril Ehrlich, Philip R. Belt, Hugh Davies, Maribel Meisel, Robert [S.] Winter, Derek Adlam, J. Bradford Robinson, William [J.] Conner, Harold C. Schonberg, Rosamond E. M. Harding, and Susan Bradshaw. *The New Grove Piano.* With a preface by Stanley Sadie. The New Grove Musical Instrument Series. New York: W. W. Norton & Company, 1988.

Parts of the book were first published in *The New Grove Dictionary of Musical Instruments*, edited by Stanley Sadie (London: Macmillan, 1984), and *The New Grove Dictionary of Music and Musicians*, also edited by Stanley Sadie (London: Macmillan, 1980). Topics include history and development of the piano, performance, performers, and literature. Chapter 1 discusses the history of the piano and contains a section dedicated to the development and modifications of the instrument Appendix 1 is a glossary of terms, most of which are related to construction and development of the piano. Appendix 2 is an index of piano makers. Photographs, illustrations (many detailed and labeled). Bibliography. 190 pp.

28. Sadie, Stanley, ed. *The New Grove Dictionary of Music and Musicians*. 20 vols. London: Macmillan, 1980. S.v. "Pianoforte," by Edwin [M.] Ripin, Philip R. Belt, Maribel Meisel, Derek Adlam, William J. Conner, Rosamond E. M. Harding, Cyril Ehrlich, and Frank Dawes.

Section 1: the history and development of the instrument, from Cristofori's pianos to the modern grands. Topics include piano builders, important inventions, and construction. Significant regional developments and constructional differences are addressed. Section 2: discusses piano playing and players. Photographs, illustrations (many labeled). Bibliography.

29. ———, ed. *The New Grove Dictionary of Musical Instruments*. London: Macmillan, 1984.

In three volumes. Topics include instruments, makers and manufacturers, and accessories and attachments. Instruments range from historical to modern, Western to non-Western, art to folk and popular instruments. Some articles are reprinted from *The New Grove Dictionary of Music and Musicians*, also edited by Stanley Sadie (London: Macmillan, 1980; 20 vols.). An entry may discuss construction, history, performance, and may include biographical information, photographs, illustrations, and bibliographies. Also see *The New Grove Dictionary of Music and Musicians*.

30. Schulz, Ferdinand F. *Pianographie: Klavierbibliographie der lieferbaren Bücher und Periodica sowie der Dissertationen in deutscher, englischer, französischer und italienischer Sprache*. Recklinghausen, Germany: Piano-Verlag, 1982.

A selective unannotated bibliography on the piano. The table of contents is in German and in English; the items included are books, periodicals (not individual articles), and dissertations, and may be in German, French, English, or Italian. Topics include composers, literature, performance, performers, piano making, miscellaneous subjects, and periodicals. The section on piano making contains over 200 items (130 are in English) and addresses history, piano technology, as well as tuning and temperament. Also included in this section are works on harpsichords, clavichords, and player pianos. Related photographs and illustrations. 458 pp.

31. Siepmann, Jeremy. *The Piano*. London: Carlton Books, 1996.

A general information book about the instrument. Topics include history, construction, literature, performance, and form and style. [Note: this is a different book from another book of the same title by the same author, published by Alfred A. Knopf in 1997.] Photographs, illustrations. 192 pp.

32. Smith, Eric. *Pianos in Practice*. London: Scolar Press, 1978.

A practical and introductory manual on pianos. In three parts. Part 1 covers general information about the piano, including distinctive features of the instrument, tone and touch, volume, history and evolution of the instrument, and purchasing a piano. Part 2 discusses general construction as well as the individual parts. Part 3 addresses maintenance, including tuning, voicing, problems, and adjustments. Photographs, illustrations (many labeled). Bibliography. 100 pp.

33. Stoddard, Hope. "Piano in the Home, Studio, Concert Hall." *International Musician* 49, no. 9 (March 1951): 20–21.

An introductory article about the piano. Addresses history, construction, literature, and other miscellaneous topics.

34. *Tuners' Journal*. Rockville, Md.: National Association of Piano Tuners.

Serial (monthly), 1921–1957. Merged with *Piano Technician*

to continue as *Piano Technicians Journal*. Topics include construction and design, tuning, maintenance and care, repairing, rebuilding, refinishing, tools and materials, problem diagnosis, dealing and trading, and business aspects of tuner-technicians.

35. Unger-Hamilton, Clive. *Keyboard Instruments*. The Covent Garden Music Guides, no. 1. Minneapolis, Minn.: Control Data Publishing, 1981.

An introductory book on the history, construction, literature, and performers of keyboard instruments (organ, harpsichord, and piano). Part 1 is dedicated to the history and construction, with a section on the social history of the piano and a section on the instrument itself. Photographs, illustrations. The glossary includes few relevant terms. 124 pp.

36. Wier, Albert E[rnest]. *The Piano: Its History, Makers, Players and Music*. London: Longmans, Green and Co., 1940.

Discusses the history, construction, literature, technique, performance, and pedagogy. Addresses grands, uprights, and player pianos. Includes a list of piano manufacturers. Bibliography, biographical dictionary of pianists, and discography. 467 pp.

# History

## General History

37. Badura-Skoda, Paul. "Instruments: Pianist's View." *Music and Musicians* 17, no. 6 (February 1969): 42–43, 70; no. 7 (March 1969): 44–45, 78; no. 8 (April 1969): 32–33.

    A series of articles about the history of the piano from a performer's point of view. Topics include construction and development, difference between Viennese and English early pianos, types of actions, and compass.

38. Banowetz, Joseph. *The Pianist's Guide to Pedaling*. Bloomington: Indiana University Press, 1985.

    Although the focus is on the use of the pedals, a short chapter about the history of the pedals is included. Bibliography. 309 pp.

39. Bie, Oscar. *A History of the Pianoforte and Pianoforte Players*. Translated and revised by E. E. Kellett and E. W. Naylor. London: J. M. Dent and Sons; New York: E. P. Dutton and Co., 1899. Reprint, with a foreword by Aube Tzerko. Da Capo Press Music Titles, ed. Frederick Freedman. New York: Da Capo Press, 1966.

    Originally in German. From the editors' preface: "This work does not profess to be so much a literal translation as a somewhat free version of Dr. Bie's 'Das Klavier.'" While the focus is on the history of piano literature, performance practice, and players, the history and development of the instrument are also discussed. Photographs, illustrations. 336 pp.

40.  Bilson, Malcolm. "Pianos in Mozart's Time (Revisited)." *Piano Quarterly* 22, no. 86 (Summer 1974): 29–31.

An introductory article about eighteenth-century pianos. Discusses the action, the pedal, and stops available on some instruments. Illustrations.

41.  ———. "The Soft Pedal Revisited." *Piano Quarterly* 30, no. 117 (Spring 1982): 36–38.

Discusses the history, construction, and function of the *una corda* pedal. Also discusses the "*celeste* stop" found on some pianos from the early nineteenth century.

42.  Blom, Eric. *The Romance of the Piano*. London: Foulis, 1928. Reprint, Da Capo Press Music Reprint Series, ed. Frederick Freedman. New York: Da Capo Press, 1969.

A history of the piano from the musical instruments of ancient civilizations to the pianos of the early twentieth century. Discusses construction and development, builders, and literature. Photographs, illustrations. Includes an illustration titled "The Genealogy of the Piano." Bibliography. 241 pp.

43.  *The Book of Complete Information about Pianos*. 15th rev. ed. New York: Frank L. Wing, 1914.

In two parts. Part 1 addresses the history and construction of the piano. Discusses types of pianos, materials used, piano parts, the construction process, sound, and basic maintenance of the piano. Part 2 includes an illustrated catalog of Wing & Son pianos, as well as other promotional materials. Illustrations (some are labeled). 131 pp.

44.  Bretzfelder, Maurice Krakauer. *The Story of the Piano*. New York: Krakauer Brothers, 1960.

Primarily intended for promotional use by the Krakauer Brothers. A booklet tracing the development of the piano from the Chinese Ke through the monochord, clavichord, spinet, clavicytherium, harpsichord, dulcimer, early piano, and square pianos, to the modern grand and vertical pianos. Several models of pianos by Krakauer Brothers are described. Photographs, illustrations. 25 pp., unpaginated.

45. Brinsmead, Edgar. *The History of the Pianoforte: With an Account of the Theory of Sound and Also of the Music and Musical Instruments of the Ancients.* London: Novello, Ewer & Co., 1879. Reprint, Detroit: Singing Tree Press, 1969.

Discusses the history and development of the piano. Also includes introductory chapters on acoustics and a short chapter on selecting and maintaining a piano. The appendices include a list of piano patents in Britain between 1693 and 1879, with their dates. Illustrations. 201 pp.

46. Buchner, Alexander. *Musical Instruments: An Illustrated History.* Translated by Borek Vancura. New York: Crown, 1973.

A general history of musical instruments from prehistoric to modern instruments. Includes comments about the piano. Photographs include those of several historical pianos. Bibliography. 274 pp.

47. ———. *Musical Instruments through the Ages.* Translated by Iris Urwin. London: Spring Books, [1956].

A general history of the musical instruments from ancient civilizations to modern times, including the piano. Several Czech piano makers are mentioned. A "family tree" of musical instruments. Photographs, illustrations. 42 pp., plus 323 plates.

48. Burnett, Richard. "Classical Keyboard." *Music and Musicians* 19, no. 5 (January 1971): 20–21.

An essay about the early pianos. Includes comments on construction. Photographs.

49. Clark, Walter Jerry. "The World's First Piano." *Clavier* 14, no. 1 (January 1975): 38–41.

Discusses a ninth-century Persian hammered dulcimer as a

forerunner to the piano. Comparisons with the modern piano. Photograph, illustration.

50. Closson, Ernest. *History of the Piano*. Translated by Delano Ames. London: Paul Elek, 1947. Reprint, St. Clair Shores, Mich.: Scholarly Press, 1977.

Originally published in French by Editions Universitaires. A history of the piano from its origins in the clavichord and the harpsichord. Discusses piano builders and construction. The appendix contains illustrations and explanations of various actions. Photographs. Bibliography. 168 pp.

51. Clutton, Cecil. "The Pianoforte." In *Musical Instruments through the Ages*, ed. Anthony Baines, 83–96. New York: Walker and Company, 1966.

An overview of the history of the instrument. Photographs, illustrations. Glossary, bibliography.

52. Cole, Michael. *The Pianoforte in the Classical Era*. New York: Oxford University Press; Oxford, England: Clarendon Press, 1998.

A history of the piano from about 1760 to 1820. Includes chapters on construction, touch and tone in the early piano, and fakes and forgeries. Appendix 1: selected passages from early sources (some in German with English translation); appendix 2: the author's proposal for the systematic classification of piano actions; appendix 3: an inventory of Americus Backers' house and workshop. Glossary, bibliography. Photographs, illustrations, tables. 398 pp.

53. Colt, C. F. "Early Pianos: Their History and Character." *Early Music* 1, no. 1 (January–February 1973): 27–33.

Discusses the development of early pianos. Descriptions of two unsigned pianos as well as pianos by Broadwood, Haxby, Heilmann, and Pape. Photographs.

54. Crombie, David. *Piano*. 1st American ed. San Francisco: Miller

Freeman Books, 1995.

A photographic history of the piano, from the ancient stringed instruments to the modern grand and upright pianos. Discusses construction, builders and manufacturers, and some maintenance and tuning of the modern piano. Also addresses electric pianos, electronic pianos, and automatic pianos. Includes a chronology, a list of piano manufacturers with brief descriptions, a discography, and a glossary. Illustrations. Bibliography. 112 pp.

55. Doerschuk, Robert L. "Piano History: Landmark Dates in the History of the Piano." *Keyboard* 19, no. 12 (December 1993): 37–45.

A chronological list of events related to the development of the piano and the piano industry, from Cristofori's first piano at the beginning of the eighteenth century to the present (1993). This is an updated and expanded version of "Landmarks in Piano History: The Unfolding of the Grand Design," *Keyboard* 14, no. 8 (August 1988): 50, 52–54, by the same author.

56. Dolge, Alfred. *Pianos and Their Makers: A Comprehensive History of the Development of the Piano from the Monochord to the Concert Grand Player Piano.* Covina, Calif.: Covina Publishing Company, 1911. Reprint, New York: Dover Publications, 1972.

In five parts. Part 1, "Technical Development of the Pianoforte." Discusses the history and evolution of the piano from the monochord to the modern pianos, including grands, uprights, squares, and player pianos. Topics include builders, construction, and the supply industry. Part 2, "Commercial Development of the Piano Industry." Topics include the industry by country, commercialism and its influence on the instruments, marketing and trade, and the trust movement in the late nineteenth century. Part 3, "Men Who Have Made Piano History." Discusses piano makers and inventors, arranged by country. Part 4, "Influence of Piano Virtuosos upon the Industry." About composers and pianists who influenced the development of the piano, with their comments about pianos. Part 5 includes short chapters on organizations of manufacturers and dealers, and the impact of journals and the press on the piano industry, as well as concluding remarks and a bibliographical essay. The appendix lists piano manufacturers and suppliers (active as of the original publication date), organized by country. [Part 3 of this book has been published separately: *Pianos and Their Makers*, vol. 2, *Development of the Piano Industry in America since the Centennial Exhibition at Philadelphia, 1876*, Covina, Calif.: Covina Publishing Company, 1913; reprint, Vestal, N.Y.: Vestal Press, 1980.] Photographs and detailed illustrations. 478 pp.

57.  Dolmetsch, Arnold. "The History of the Piano." *Morning Post* (London), 22 July 1901, p. 2.

A brief history of the piano. Discusses its development, the escapements, and types of pianos.

58.  Edwards, Miriam. "Pedal for Pianists." *American Music Teacher* 23, no. 5 (April–May 1974): 18–20.

The history of piano pedals. Includes the standard pedals found on the modern piano and other pedals found on earlier instruments. Bibliography.

59.  Ehrlich, Cyril. *The Piano: A History*. Rev. ed. Oxford, England: Clarendon Press, 1990.

First published in 1976 by J. M. Dent and Sons. A history of the piano, with a focus after the mid-nineteenth century. Discusses the industry and the instrument itself. Appendix 1: a list of piano builders since 1851 organized by country, with dates; appendix 2: estimates of piano production volume from 1850 to 1985 by country; appendix 3: a brief article on exotic or unusual pianos. Photographs, tables, and graphs. Bibliography. 254 pp.

60.  ———. *Social Emulation and Industrial Progress: The Victorian Piano*. Queen's University of Belfast New Lecture Series, vol. 82. [Belfast, Ireland]: by the author, 1975.

Discusses the piano industry during the nineteenth century. Topics include manufacturers, production, and distribution. An inaugural lecture given at the Queen's University of Belfast on February 5, 1975. Illustration. Bibliography. 20 pp.

61.  Eisenberg, Jacob. "A Thumbnail Pictorial History of the Piano." *Musical Courier* 142, no. 4 (September 1950): 22–23.

An illustrated outline of the history of the piano, from mythological legends to the modern piano. Each illustration or photograph is accompanied by a short caption that explains the significance of the event, invention, or person in the development of the piano.

62.  Engel, Carl. *A Descriptive Catalogue of the Musical Instruments in the South Kensington Museum, Preceded by an Essay on the History of Musical Instruments.* 2nd ed. London: Chapman & Hall, 1874. Reprint, New York: Benjamin Blom, 1971.

In two parts. The first part is an overview of the history of musical instruments from prehistoric times. The second part contains brief descriptions of the musical instruments (including several pianos) at the museum, most of which are not accompanied by illustrations or photographs. The first appendix contains descriptions of instruments (including several pianos) on loan to the museum. The second appendix contains accounts of the special exhibition of ancient musical instruments at the museum in 1872. 402 pp.

63.  Epstein, Abraham. "The Stick, the Log, and the String." *American Music Teacher* 12, no. 6 (July–August 1963): 18, 35.

An introductory overview of the evolution of the piano tracing the development of musical instruments from primitive percussion instruments through the monochord and early stringed keyboard instruments to the modern piano.

64.  "Evolution of the Grand Piano." *Music Journal* 19, no. 2 (February 1961): 48–49. Reprint, *Music Journal* 29, no. 2 (February 1971): 84–85.

An introductory article about the development of stringed keyboard instruments leading up to the piano. Photographs.

65.  Fleming, William Coleman. "The Relation of the Pianoforte to the Romantic Movement in Music." M.A. thesis, Claremont Colleges, 1939.

While the main text focuses on the Romantic musical style, the appendix contains three articles about the piano: the development of the piano, well temperament, and the development of the piano pedals. In addition, table 1 is a chronological list of significant events in the development of the piano, and table 2 is a list of compasses of some early keyboard instruments. Bibliography. 106 pp.

66.  Frederick, Edmund M[ichael]. "The 'Romantic' Sound in Four Pianos of Chopin's Era." *19th Century Music* 3, no. 2 (November 1979): 150–53.

Brief descriptions of four typical grand pianos from 1820 to 1860. Focuses on the sound from the performer's perspective.

67.  Fuller, Luther Marion. "The History and Development of the Piano." M.A. thesis, Boston University, 1924.

An overview of the history of the piano from the monochord to the modern piano. Discusses square pianos, uprights, grands, and player pianos. Also addresses pedals. Bibliography. 31 pp.

68.  Galpin, Francis W. *A Textbook of European Musical Instruments: Their Origin, History, and Character.* London: Ernest Benn, 1956. Reprint, Westport, Conn.: Greenwood Press, 1976.

A general history and construction of musical instruments including pianos (under chordophonic instruments). Includes a list of collections of musical instruments. Photographs (no pianos), illustrations. Bibliography. 256 pp.

69.  Gates, Robert Edward. "The Influence of the Eighteenth-Century Piano on the Music of Joseph Haydn." D.M. thesis, Indiana University, 1982.

Includes background information about the early Viennese and English pianos (construction, development, sound, pedals, etc.)

and Haydn's relationship with the pianos. Illustrations (some labeled). Bibliography. 148 pp.

70. Gates, Willey Francis. *Pipe and Strings: Three Historic and Descriptive Sketches: The Origin and Development of the Organ, the Evolution of the Pianoforte, the Violin and Its Ancestry.* Cincinnati: John Church Co., 1895.

Especially see "The Evolution of the Pianoforte," pp. 31–63: Traces the development of the instrument from ancient instruments to the modern piano, addressing builders and construction. Illustrations. 107 pp.

71. Gaumer, Samuel B. "The Modern Piano." *Etude* 68, no. 3 (March 1950): 10–11.

A brief essay about the history of the piano. Illustrations.

72. Geiringer, Karl. *Instruments in the History of Western Music.* 3rd rev. and enl. ed. New York: Oxford University Press, 1978.

A textbook on the history of musical instruments including pianos. Previous editions were published under the title *Musical Instruments.* See *Musical Instruments: Their History in Western Culture from the Stone Age to the Present Day*, translated by Bernard Miall, edited by W. F. H. Blandford (New York: Oxford University Press, 1945) by the same author. Photographs, illustrations. Bibliography. 318 pp.

73. Gillespie, John. *Five Centuries of Keyboard Music: An Historical Survey of Music for Harpsichord and Piano.* Belmont, Calif.: Wadsworth Publishing Company, 1965. Reprint, New York: Dover Publications, 1972.

While the book focuses on the piano literature, it includes a chapter on the history and development of the piano. Photographs, illustrations. Glossary of musical terms, bibliography. 463 pp.

74. Glover, Ellye Howell. *How the Piano Came to Be.* Chicago: Browne & Howell Company, 1913.

Traces the history of the piano from the ancient stringed instruments to the modern piano. Photographs, illustrations. 60 pp.

75. Golightly, John Wesley. "The Piano between 1800 and 1850: The Instruments for Which the Composers Wrote." D.M.A. document, Ohio State University, 1980.

An overview of early piano technology. Discusses construction of the piano and its effects on performance. Selected piano builders are organized into Viennese, English, and French builders. Also discusses piano ideals of Beethoven, Schubert, Chopin, Mendelssohn, and Schumann. Illustrations (some labeled). Bibliography. 118 pp.

76. Good, Edwin M. *Giraffes, Black Dragons, and Other Pianos: A Technological History from Cristofori to the Modern Concert Grand.* Stanford: Stanford University Press, 1982.

A history of piano construction and technology. Also discusses experimental pianos, electric and electronic pianos, and automation of the piano. Photographs, illustrations. Bibliography. 305 pp.

77. Gough, Hugh. "The Classical Grand Pianoforte, 1770–1830." *Proceedings of the Royal Musical Association* 77 (1950–1951): 41–50.

Discusses the technical problems faced by the early piano makers and their solutions, differences between Viennese pianos and English pianos of the time, and other constructional developments.

78. Gough, Patricia K. "The Piano and Its Music: A Cultural History." M.A. thesis, San Jose State University, 1983.

An introduction to the development of the piano and its music, intended for high school classes or other beginner audiences. A slide show (two carrousels) with recorded musical examples (two 45-minute cassette tapes). The text contains the narrator's scripts, study guides, lists and facsimiles of the slides. Bibliography. 134 pp.

79. Grame, Theodore. "The Piano in Mozart's Time." *American Music Teacher* 12, no. 6 (July–August 1963): 19, 34.

An overview of pianos from the eighteenth century.

80. "A Grand Piano Is Born—A Story of Art and Industry." *Musical America* 77, no. 3 (February 1957): 13–15, 92.

A short article about the history of the grand piano. Includes photographs of various stages of grand piano building at the Baldwin factory in Cincinnati, with explanatory captions.

81. Grover, David S. *A History of the Piano from 1709–1980.* Macclesfield, England: Omicron, 1980.

Traces the constructional changes of the piano from Cristofori's instrument to the modern vertical pianos, discussing major developments. Photographs, illustrations (labeled). 16 pp.

82. ———. *The Piano: Its Story, from Zither to Grand.* New York: Charles Scribner's Sons, 1978.

Traces the history of the piano from the primitive instruments to the modern pianos. Discusses construction and its relationship to piano music. Includes a chronological list of important events in the development of the piano. Bibliography. Photographs, illustrations. 223 pp.

83. Guenther, Felix. *The Piano and Its Ancestors: Aid Material for Music Appreciation Studies.* With a foreword by Louis G. Wersen. New York: Sound Book Press Society, 1950.

A textbook on the history of keyboard instruments from harpsichord and clavichord to the modern piano. Discusses general construction, literature, and the social history of the instruments. Photographs, illustrations. Bibliography. 56 pp.

84. Halfpenny, Eric. "The Later History of the 'Square.'" *Musical Opinion* 64, no. 758 (November 1940): 90–91.

Discusses the construction of the square pianos made between 1800 and 1820. Topics include compass, action, pedals, stringing,

1800 and 1820. Topics include compass, action, pedals, stringing, and cabinetry.

85.   Harding, Rosamond [E. M.]. "Experimental Pianofortes and the Music Written for Them." *Proceedings of the [Royal] Musical Association* 57 (1930–1931): 57–71.

Topics include devices for sustaining sound, octave couplers, stops, experimental repetition actions, and instruments that combine piano and another instrument.

86.   ————. *The Pianoforte: Its History Traced to the Great Exhibition of 1851.* 2nd and rev. ed. Old Woking, England: Gresham Books, 1978.

Originally published in 1933. A history of the piano from the beginning of the eighteenth century to the mid-nineteenth century. Discusses developments in Italy, France, Germany, England, and America. Topics include musical significance of the instrument, the evolution of the instrument and musical influences on the evolution, types of pianos, miscellaneous parts (such as octave couplers, swells, and stops) and experimental pianos, pitch and temperament, and general maintenance. Appendices include a glossary of technical terms in four languages (English, American, German, and French), a list of patents (arranged by parts), a list of piano scales, articles on hammerheads (most in French or German), a list of piano prices and materials used in piano making, a selective list of piano builders in London and vicinity from 1760 to 1851, and a short article on pedal signs. Photographs, illustrations (many labeled). Bibliography. 450 pp.

87.   Harrison, Sidney. *Grand Piano*. London: Faber and Faber, 1976.

A history of the piano. Discusses construction and development, builders and inventors, composers, and performers. Photographs, illustrations. 272 pp.

88.   Henrickson, Donald Gene. "The Harpsichord and the Development of the Piano Prior to the Lieder of Schubert." D.M.A. thesis, University of Missouri, Kansas City, 1970.

Traces the development of the piano from the harpsichord to the early nineteenth century, particularly from the perspective of an accompanist. Illustrations. Bibliography. 77 pp.

89.  Hess, Albert G. "The Transition from Harpsichord to Piano." *Galpin Society Journal* no. 6 (July 1953): 75–94.

Discusses the use of harpsichord and piano during the early phase in piano history. Examines the original titles of works with keyboard published in England during the second half of the eighteenth century and studies a collection of confiscated pianos and harpsichords in France during the French Revolution.

90.  Hildebrandt, Dieter. *Pianoforte: A Social History of the Piano.* Translated by Harriet Goodman. With an introduction by Anthony Burgess. New York: George Braziller, 1988.

Originally in German. A compilation of stories and events surrounding pianos, pianists, composers, and piano builders, primarily in continental Europe. 207 pp.

91.  Hipkins, Alfred J[ames]. *A Description and History of the Pianoforte and of the Older Stringed Keyboard Instruments.* 3rd ed. Novello's Music Primers and Educational Series. London: Novello, 1929. Reprint, with an introduction by Edwin M. Ripin. Detroit Reprints in Music. Detroit: Information Coordinators, 1975.

In three parts. Part 1 discusses the modern piano since the introduction of the cast-iron plate (after about 1820). Addresses various piano parts (wrest plank, case and frame, soundboard, bridges, action, strings, and pedals), the strike points, and tuning. Part 2 discusses keyboard instruments before the birth of the piano, including clavichords, virginals, clavicytheriums, harpsichords, organized spinets, and others up to the year 1800. Part 3 discusses the early piano up to the introduction of the cast-iron plate, covering the years 1709 to about 1820. Illustrations (some labeled). Glossary. 130 pp.

92.  Hirt, Franz Josef. *Stringed Keyboard Instruments, 1440–1880.*

Translated by M. Boehme-Brown. Boston: Boston Book and Art Shop, 1968. Reprint, Dietikton-Zürich, Germany: Urs Graf Verlag, 1981.

German title: *Meisterwerke des Klavierbaus*. Originally published in German in 1958. Part 1: photographs and descriptions of historical instruments with relic values. Part 2: construction and history of keyboard instruments. Part 3: descriptions of categories based on construction. Part 4: descriptions of specific instruments, including dates, signatures, constructions, and current locations. Appendix: a chronological list of leading builders of stringed keyboard instruments until 1880, organized by country. In German and in English. Includes a list of museums and private collections of musical instruments. Photographs, illustrations (many labeled). Bibliography. 235 pp.

93.  Hollis, Helen Rice. *The Musical Instruments of Joseph Haydn: An Introduction*. With a foreword by H. C. Robbins Landon. Smithsonian Studies in History and Technology, no. 38. Washington, D.C.: Smithsonian Institution Press, 1977.

Discusses the musical instruments of Haydn's time, his experiences, and his use of the instruments. The section on keyboards discusses Haydn's preferences and experiences, with photographs and brief descriptions of surviving instruments. Also discusses instrumentation in Haydn's works. Bibliography. 33 pp.

94.  ———. *The Piano: A Pictorial Account of Its Ancestry and Development*. New and rev. ed. New York: Hippocrene Books, 1984.

A history of the piano from the ancient instruments to the modern piano. Discusses construction, social history, performance, and literature. Photographs, facsimiles, illustrations (many labeled). Bibliography. 130 pp.

95.  ———. *The Pianos in the Smithsonian Institution*. Smithsonian Studies in History and Technology, no. 27. Washington, D.C.: Smithsonian Institution Press, 1973.

Outlines the history of the piano, accompanied by photographs and descriptions of selected instruments at the Smithsonian Institution. Instruments range from the predecessors of the piano to the White House Steinway. Photographs and illustrations of the actions are labeled. Bibliography. 47 pp.

96. Houck, Margaret A. "The History and Development of the Sostenuto Pedal and Its Use in Selected 20th-Century Repertoire." M.M. thesis, California State University, Fullerton, 1982.

A history of the piano pedals, especially of the sostenuto pedal. Discusses functions, mechanisms, and use. Bibliography. 54 pp.

97. James, Philip [Brutton]. *Early Keyboard Instruments: From Their Beginnings to the Year 1820*. [London: P. Davies; London: Holland Press; New York: Stokes, 1930.] Reprint, New York: Barnes & Noble, 1970.

Originally published in 1930. A history of the stringed keyboard instruments, including the piano. The appendix is a list of builders and sellers of stringed keyboard instruments who worked in the British Isles up to the year 1820 (including resident foreigners), with their addresses, dates of known existence, and additional remarks. Photographs (with detailed captions), illustrations (labeled). Bibliography. 153 pp.

98. Kelley, Edgar Stillman. *Musical Instruments*. Boston: Oliver Ditson; New York: Charles H. Ditson & Co.; Chicago: Lyon & Healy; London: Winthrop Rogers, 1925.

A textbook about the history of musical instruments. The chapter on the piano and its predecessors discusses general construction, temperament, literature, and performance. Photographs. 243 pp.

99. Kendall, Alan. *The World of Musical Instruments*. London: Hamlyn, 1972.

A general history of musical instruments. A chapter is dedicated to keyboard instruments, including the piano (under stringed keyboard instruments). Photographs, illustrations. 128 pp.

100. Krehbiel, Henry Edward. *A Lecture by Mr. H. E. Krehbiel on "The Precursors of the Pianoforte" with Illustrative Music . . . .* [New York]: N.p., [1890].

Booklet. Two versions: one for a lecture dated May 2, 1890, at Steinway Hall in New York; another for a lecture dated May 13, 1890, at Steinert Hall in Boston. A collection of illustrations outlining the evolution of the keyboard instrument up to the grand piano of the day. The May 13 version includes illustrations of examples of keyboard instruments in M. Steinert's collection. 12 pp. (May 2nd version); 15 pp. (May 13th version).

101. ———. *The Pianoforte and Its Music.* The Music Lover's Library. New York: C. Scribner's Sons, 1911. Reprint, Portland, Maine: Longwood Press, 1976.

Discusses the history, construction, literature, and performers of the piano. Part 1 is dedicated to the history and construction from the ancient instruments to the modern piano. Photographs, illustrations. 314 pp.

102. Latcham, Michael. "The Check in Some Early Pianos and the Development of Piano Technique around the Turn of the 18th Century." *Early Music* 21, no. 1 (February 1993): 28–42.

A history of the check and the action. Includes a table of the dates of the instruments mentioned in the text. Photographs, illustrations (labeled).

103. Leppert, Richard. "Sexual Identity, Death, and the Family Piano." *19th Century Music* 16, no. 2 (Fall 1992): 105–28.

Discusses parallels between the social views about the piano and about women in the nineteenth century. Photographs.

104. Libin, Laurence. "The Instruments." In *Eighteenth-Century Keyboard Music*, edited by Robert L. Marshall, 1–32. New York: Macmillan, Schirmer Books, 1994.

A detailed article about various keyboard instruments of the eighteenth century including pianos. Topics include use of these instruments, social and cultural aspects, manufacturing, and construction. Discusses the harpsichord, the clavichord, the piano, and the organ in detail; also discusses carillons and other keyboard instruments from the century. Photographs. Bibliography.

105. ———. *Keynotes: Two Centuries of Piano Design.* New York: Metropolitan Museum of Art, 1985.

Traces the development of the piano through descriptions of selected pianos at the Metropolitan Museum of Art. Includes grands, squares, uprights, pedal pianos, and other miscellaneous pianos. An entry may include information about the builder, dates, construction, compass, other background information, and illustrations. 48 pp., unpaginated.

106. Loesser, Arthur. *Men, Women, and Pianos: A Social History.* With a preface by Jacques Barzun. New York: Simon and Schuster, 1954. Reprint, with a foreword by Edward Rothstein. New York: Dover Publications, 1990.

Discusses the history and development of the piano and its industry, people who influenced the development of the piano, and the social and cultural history as reflected by the piano. Arranged by country, concluded by a chapter on general developments. Bibliography. 654 pp.

107. Marcuse, Sibyl. *Musical Instruments: A Comprehensive Dictionary.* Garden City, N.Y.: Doubleday & Company, 1964.

"Piano," pp. 402–6. A brief summary of the history, construction, and development of the piano. Discusses important inventors and builders. Also see "Fortepiano," p. 192.

108. ———. *A Survey of Musical Instruments.* New York: Harper & Row, 1975.

A general history of musical instruments, arranged by category. The piano is discussed in part 3 ("Chordophones") under the heading "Keyboard Chordophones." Traces the history of the piano from the harpsichord, by country. Addresses double pianos, square pianos, upright pianos, and grand pianos. Also included are harpsichord-pianos, tangent pianos, sustaining pianos, pedal pianos, enharmonic pianos, and player pianos. Photographs (none of the piano), illustrations. Glossary, bibliography. 863 pp.

109. Mason, Henry L[owell]. *How Has the Pianoforte as an Instrument Developed since 1876? And Some Figures.* N.p., 1928.

An address given by the president of Mason & Hamlin at the Music Teachers National Association meeting in Cleveland, Ohio; originally published in the proceedings for 1928. A history of the piano with a focus on the development from the late nineteenth century to the early twentieth century. 15 pp.

110. Miller, Samuel D. "W. Otto Miessner's Small Upright Piano: Its Invention, History, and Influence on the Piano Industry." *American Music Teacher* 29, no. 5 (April–May 1980): 24–26.

A history of the modern spinet piano from Miessner's invention of the instrument.

111. Mobbs, Kenneth. "Stops and Other Special Effects on the Early Piano." *Early Music* 12, no. 4 (November 1984): 471–76.

Discusses stops and controls on the early piano such as standard pedals (the sustaining pedal, the shift pedal, among others), bassoon and percussion stops (Janissary stops), and other special effects. Discusses advantages and disadvantages of handstops, kneestops, and foot-operated stops. Examples drawn mostly from the author's collection of instruments. Photographs.

112. Montagu, Jeremy. *The World of Baroque & Classical Musical Instruments.* Woodstock, N.Y.: Overlook Press, 1979.

A general history of musical instruments. Includes keyboard instruments up to the early piano. Photographs. Bibliography. 136 pp.

113. ———. *The World of Romantic & Modern Musical Instruments.* Woodstock, N.Y.: Overlook Press, 1981.

A general history of musical instruments. A chapter is dedicated to keyboard instruments which includes the nineteenth-century piano to the modern pianos. Photographs. Bibliography. 136 pp.

114. "Music Trade Forum: Appearances." *Musical Opinion* 88, no. 1048 (January 1965): 253.

Discusses changes in the upright piano market and some factors that contributed to the changes in appearance of upright pianos.

115. "Music Trade Forum: Fashions in Pianos." *Musical Opinion* 85, no. 1013 (February 1962): 317.

An essay about the decline of square pianos in favor of upright pianos.

116. "Music Trade Forum: Queer Pianos." *Musical Opinion* 85, no. 1019 (August 1962): 701.

Compares some unusual historical pianos and piano devices to their modern equivalents.

117. Newman, William S. "A Capsule History of the Piano." *American Music Teacher* 12, no. 6 (July–August 1963): 14–15.

A brief article about the history of the instrument.

118. Palmieri, Robert. "300 Years of Piano History." *Clavier* 36, no. 10 (December 1997): 16–19, 42.

A brief history of the piano. Discusses builders, construction, and composers. Photographs.

119. Parakilas, James, ed. *Piano Roles: Three Hundred Years of Life with the Piano*. With a foreword by Noah Adams. New Haven, Conn.: Yale University Press, 1999.

A collection of articles and essays about the social and cultural history of the piano. Topics include construction, marketing and merchandising, playing and performing, and the role of the piano in the lives of people. Photographs, illustrations. A bibliographical essay on recommended readings. 461 pp.

120. Parrish, Carl. "Criticisms of the Piano When It Was New." *Musical Quarterly* 30, no. 4 (October 1944): 428–40.

Concerns the transition from harpsichord to piano. Discusses the development of the piano up to the late eighteenth century, factors that affected the dissemination of the piano, and reactions to the instrument.

121. ———. "The Early Piano and Its Influence on Keyboard Technique and Composition in the Eighteenth Century." Ph.D. dissertation, Harvard University, 1939. Reprint, RMP Studies in Musicology, Series A. Superior, Wisc.: Research Microfilm Publishers, 1953.

Chapter 1 discusses the history of the piano up to its establishment within the European musical culture in the eighteenth century. Chapters 2 and 3 discuss the influence of the instrument on musical style. Bibliography. 438 pp.

122. Plante, Anne Marie. "The Iconography of the Piano in Nineteenth-Century Art." D.M. thesis, Indiana University, 1984.

In two volumes. A history of the piano as reflected in nineteenth-century visual art works. Works range from caricatures to serious portraits. Volume 1 contains the text; volume 2 contains the artwork referenced in the text. 34 pp., 51 pp.

123. Pollens, Stewart. "The Bonafinis Spinet: An Early Harpsichord Converted into a Tangent Piano." *Journal of the American Musical Instrument Society* 13 (1987): 5–22.

Examines a small pentagonal octave spinet harpsichord converted into a tangent piano, possibly in the late sixteenth century, as evidence that pianos may have been made as early as the sixteenth or the early seventeenth century. Discusses the origin and history of the instrument. Detailed description of the instrument and its construction. The appendix is a list of dimensions, string lengths, and wire sizes of the instrument. Photographs.

124. ———. *The Early Pianoforte*. Cambridge Musical Texts and Monographs. Cambridge: Cambridge University Press, 1995.

Discusses the history and construction of the piano (defined more generally as a stringed keyboard instrument with striking mechanisms) from the fifteenth century to 1763. Appendices contain primary sources in original languages, and notes from Scipione Maffei's interview with Bartolomeo Cristofori (in Italian and in English). Photographs, illustrations. Bibliography. 297 pp.

125. Ratcliffe, Ronald V. "Early Pianos: Performance Problems on Pre-1850 Instruments." *Contemporary Keyboard* 5, no. 3 (March 1979): 12–13.

Discusses the construction of early pianos and its effect on performance, particularly on technique. Photographs.

126. ———. "Pianos from the Golden Age: There's More to Craftsmanship Than Meets the Ear." *Contemporary Keyboard* 5, no. 8 (August 1979): 16–20.

A history of ornate pianos. Includes descriptions and photographs of several ornate grands and uprights.

127. ———. "Milestones or Millstones? Upright Pianos of the Past." *Keyboard* 12, no. 8 (August 1986): 82–84.

Discusses the history and construction of historical upright pianos. Photographs.

128. ———. "Where the Action Is: How It Affects the Performer." *Clavier* 17, no. 6 (September 1978): 20–22.

A brief history of the piano action and its implications for the modern performer. Labeled photographs of actions.

129. Remnant, Mary. *Musical Instruments: An Illustrated History from Antiquity to the Present*. Portland, Ore.: Amadeus Press, 1989.

Includes an overview of the history of stringed keyboard instruments. Photographs, illustration. Bibliography. 240 pp.

130. Rimbault, Edward Francis. *The Pianoforte, Its Origin, Progress, and Construction; with Some Account of Instruments of the Same Class Which Preceded It; viz. the Clavichord, the Virginal, the Spinet, the Harpsichord, etc., to Which Is Added a Selection of Interesting Specimens of Music Composed for Keyed-Stringed Instruments by Blitheman, Byrd, Bull, Frescobaldi, Dumont, Chambonières, Lully, Purcell, Muffat, Couperin, Kuhnau, Scarlatti, Seb. Bach, Mattheson, Handel, C. P. Emanuel Bach, etc.* London: R. Cocks and Co., 1860.

Discusses history and construction from the ancient stringed instruments to the nineteenth-century pianoforte. Addresses the frame, stringing, action, pedals and other sustaining devices, and other miscellaneous topics. Includes a collection of works that illustrate the development of the stringed keyboard instruments. Appendices include a glossary and articles on maintenance and repair. Illustrations (some labeled). 420 pp.

131. Rothstein, Edward. "For the Piano, Chords of Change." *New York Times*, 27 September 1987, sec. 2, pp. 1, 28.

An essay about trends in the piano market and industry. Photographs.

132. Rowland, David, ed. *The Cambridge Companion to the Piano.* Cambridge Companions to Music. Cambridge: Cambridge University Press, 1998.

A collection of articles about construction, history, performers, and literature. Part 1 addresses the instrument and pianists. Relevant articles are: 1. "The Piano to c. 1770," pp. 7–21, by David Rowland; 2. "Pianos and Pianists c. 1770–c. 1825," pp. 22–39, by David Rowland; 3. "The Piano since c. 1825," pp. 40–56, by David Rowland; and 6. "The Acoustics of the Piano," pp. 96–113, by Bernard Richardson. Photographs, illustrations. Glossary, bibliography. 244 pp.

133. ———. *A History of Pianoforte Pedalling.* Cambridge Musical Texts and Monographs. Cambridge: Cambridge University Press, 1993.

Although the focus is on the use of pedals, a section about the history of the pedals and stops is included. Bibliography. 194 pp.

134. Sachs, Curt. "The Early Fate of the Piano." *Instrumentalist* 13, no. 1 (September 1958): 44–45.

A brief article on the history of the piano up to the early nineteenth century. Photographs.

135. ———. *The History of Musical Instruments*. New York: W. W. Norton & Company, 1940.

Discusses musical instruments from prehistoric times to the twentieth century. The piano is presented in the chapter on Romanticism (1750–1900). Photographs (none of the piano), illustrations. Glossary, bibliography. 505 pp.

136. Sandor, Gyorgy. "Using the Pedals." *Keyboard Classics* 2, no. 3 (May–June 1982): 44–46; no. 4 (July–August 1982): 46–48.

Reprinted from *On Piano Playing* (Schirmer Books, 1981) by the author. The article focuses on the use of the pedals. Includes an overview of the history of the pedals.

137. Schimmel, Nikolaus. *Piano Manufacturing—An Art and a Craft*. Braunschweig, Germany: Wilhelm Schimmel Pianofortefabrik, 1990.

The first half of the book covers general history of the piano (from ancient instruments to the modern piano) and the construction and evolution of the instrument. The rest is a profile of Schimmel Piano Company and its instruments, including company history, a photographic tour of the manufacturing plant, and discussion about their research. Photographs, illustrations (some labeled). 95 pp.

138. Schott, Howard. "From Harpsichord to Pianoforte: A Chronology and Commentary." *Early Music* 13, no. 1 (February 1985): 28–38.

An article about the transition from the harpsichord to the piano. Includes a year-by-year chronology from the birth of the piano to the approximate end of the harpsichord era. Illustrations.

139. Selch, Frederick R. "The Glory of the Piano." *Ovation* 8, no. 10 (November 1987): 24–27.

A short article about the history of the piano. Includes a section concerning piano selection and purchase. Photographs, illustrations.

140. ———. "The Pianoforte Rediscovered." *Ovation* 7, no. 4 (May 1986): 26.

A short article about the evolution of the piano, from Cristofori's invention to the modern piano. A photograph of a Cristofori piano and Scipione Maffei's diagram for the Cristofori action.

141. Shead, Herbert [A.]. "Notes on the Historical Background and the Working of the Modern Piano." *Music Teacher* 54, no. 2 (February 1975): 10–11; no. 3 (March 1975): 17; no. 4 (April 1975): 16–18; no. 5 (May 1975): 21–22.

An outline of the history of the piano from the virginals, the spinet, the harpsichord, the clavichord, up to the modern piano. Also includes an overview of the construction of the modern piano, discussing the soundboard, strings, pitch, action, and pedals. Addresses differences between upright and grand pianos, other historical details, and some modern developments. Illustrations. Bibliography.

142. ———. "The Upside Down Pianoforte." *Music Teacher* 58, no. 5 (May 1979): 24–25, 28.

Discusses an experimental grand piano from the nineteenth century with the soundboard and tuning pins above the strings and the action. Includes discussions about other experimental piano constructional designs in the nineteenth century such as downstriking actions. Photograph, illustrations.

143. Siepmann, Jeremy. *The Piano*. Everyman's Library—EMI Classics Music Companions, ed. Michael Rose. New York: Alfred A. Knopf, 1997.

A general introduction to the history of the piano. Primarily discusses social history, although construction and design are discussed as well. Includes a chronology of important events in piano history. [Note: this is a different book from another book of the same title by the same author, published by Carlton Books in 1996.] Photographs, illustrations. Accompanied by three CDs. Bibliographical and discographical essays. 184 pp.

144. Smith, Fanny Morris. *A Noble Art: Three Lectures on the Evolution and Construction of the Piano.* New York: De Vinne Press, 1892.

"Evolution of the Piano" addresses the history and development of the piano. "Scientific Construction of the Piano" addresses the general construction and parts of the piano; discusses strings, action, soundboard, and bracing in detail. "The Artists of Piano-Making" addresses piano making and construction, builders, and industry. Illustrations. 160 pp.

145. Strain, Emma E. "A History of the Pianoforte." M.M. thesis, University of Kansas, 1951.

Traces the development from early keyboard instruments such as the organ, plucked string instruments such as the psaltery and the exaquier, and struck string instruments such as the monochord and the dulcimer, up to the modern grands, squares, and uprights. The final chapter discusses how the piano was received over time. Bibliography. 57 pp.

146. Strauch Brothers. *The Manufacture of Pianoforte Action: Its Rise and Development.* New York: Strauch Brothers, 1891.

In two parts. The first part discusses the history and evolution of the piano and its action. The second part discusses the manufacturing process of the modern piano action at the Strauch factory in New York. Illustrations. 61 pp.

147. Sumner, William Leslie. *The Pianoforte.* 3rd ed. London: Macdonald, 1971.

Originally published in 1966 (London: Macdonald and Co.). A

history of the piano and its music. Discusses early keyboard instruments and their transition to the piano, construction and evolution, tuning and temperament, piano builders, composers, player pianos, and other miscellaneous topics. The appendix is a list of prominent composers for keyboard instruments. Photographs, illustrations (many labeled). Bibliography. 223 pp.

148. van Barthold, Kenneth, and David Buckton. *The Story of the Piano*. London: British Broadcasting Corporation, 1975.

Traces the development of the piano from the harpsichord to the modern piano, with minimal technical details. English, Viennese, and French pianos are treated in separate chapters. The appendix illustrates Wornum's tape-check action and the repetition action. Photographs, illustrations (many labeled). 109 pp.

149. Wainwright, David. *The Piano Makers*. London: Hutchinson, 1975.

About piano builders and their instruments from the time of Cristofori. Discusses construction, business history and relations of the builders, and their relationships with musical life. Photographs, illustrations. Bibliography, discography. 192 pp.

150. "What's Inside a Piano?" *Design for Arts in Education* 83, no. 6 (July–August 1982): 18–23.

An overview of the history, construction, and development of the piano. Adapted from *The Book of the Piano*, edited by Dominic Gill (Ithaca, N.Y.: Cornell University Press, 1981). Photographs.

151. Wilson, Michael I. "The Case of the Victorian Piano." *Victoria and Albert Museum Yearbook* 3 (1972): 133–53.

Discusses the ornate and decorative piano cases and piano case designs during the Victorian era. Grand and upright examples. Photographs, illustrations.

152. Winter, Robert S. "Striking It Rich: The Significance of Striking Points in the Evolution of the Romantic Piano." *Journal of Musi-*

*cology* 6, no. 3 (Summer 1988): 267–92.

Concerns pianistic ideals of tone color during the Romantic era and their effect on the development of the instrument, particularly on the strike points. Illustrations.

153. Winternitz, Emanuel. *Keyboard Instruments in the Metropolitan Museum of Art: A Picture Book.* New York: Metropolitan Museum of Art, 1961.

A selective photographic catalog of the historical keyboard instruments at the museum, including eight pianos. Brief descriptions of the instruments with origins and dates. Traces the history of keyboard instruments through the selections. 48 pp.

154. ———. *Musical Instruments of the Western World.* New York: McGraw-Hill Books, [1967].

A history of musical instruments. Discusses literature, classification, and issues in collecting instruments. Photographs and descriptions of musical instruments from the sixth century B.C. to the mid-nineteenth century, including a grand piano by Erard and other stringed keyboard instruments. Illustrations. Bibliography. 259 pp.

155. Wolfram, Victor. *The Sostenuto Pedal.* Arts and Science Studies: Humanities Series, no. 8. Stillwater: Oklahoma State University, 1965.

A history of the sostenuto pedal and its use. Traces the history of the selective sustaining concept from a 1767 piano by Zumpe. 45 pp.

156. Yamaha International Corporation (Nippon Gakki Seizo Kabushiki Kaisha). *All about Yamaha Piano.* Hamamatsu, Japan: by the company, [1979].

In two parts. The first part is a brief history of the piano, from Cristofori to the modern piano. The second part is a photographic tour of the Yamaha piano manufacturing plant. Primarily intended as a company profile. 53 pp.

157. Zaslaw, Neal. "Mozart's Instruments: Introduction." *Early Music* 20, no. 1 (February 1992): 5–6.

Compares the regional preferences for different orchestral instruments to those of pianos around Mozart's time. Summarizes differences between the Viennese and the English fortepianos.

158. Zilberquit [Zilberkvit], Mark [Aleksandrovich]. *The Book of the Piano: An Illustrated History.* Trans. by Yuri S. Shirokov. Neptune, N.J.: Paganiniana Publications, 1987.

Originally in Russian. Traces the evolution of the instrument from the monochord to the late nineteenth-century pianos. Photographs, illustrations. 79 pp.

## Australia

159. Crisp, Deborah. "The Piano in Australia, 1770 to 1900: Some Literary Sources." *Musicology Australia* 18 (1995): 25–38.

Discusses the social and cultural history of the piano in Australia. Examines letters, diaries, novels, and other accounts, in addition to secondary sources. Bibliography.

## Austria and Germany

160. Badura-Skoda, Eva. "Prolegomena to a History of the Viennese Fortepiano." *Israel Studies in Musicology* 2 (1980): 77–99.

A history of the piano in eighteenth-century and early nineteenth-century Vienna, including the first concert use of the fortepiano. Facsimiles.

161. ———. "The Viennese Fortepiano in the Eighteenth Century." In *Music in Eighteenth-Century Austria*, ed. David Wyn Jones, 249–58. New York: Cambridge University Press, 1996.

Topics include the availability of the fortepiano in the early eighteenth-century Vienna, transition instruments from harpsichord to piano, compound instruments with piano, and devices such as stops and pedals. Attempts to correct some misconceptions about the early history of the fortepiano in Vienna.

162. Bilson, Malcolm. "Schubert's Piano Music and the Pianos of His Time." *Studia Musicologica* 22, nos. 1–4 (1980): 263–71.

An essay about Viennese fortepiano and performance of works by Schubert. Reprinted in *Piano Quarterly* 27, no. 104 (Winter 1978–1979): 56–61; and in *Piano Quarterly* 40, no. 158 (Summer 1992): E11–E13.

163. Cole, Michael. "*Tafelklaviere* in the Germanisches National-museum: Some Preliminary Observations." *Galpin Society Journal* no. 50 (March 1997): 180–207.

A study of the square pianos at the museum in Nuremberg. Categorizes pre-1790 square pianos into four types by shape and action. The appendix contains summary descriptions of some instruments at the museum. Illustrations.

164. Dahl, Christine. "Early Pianos and Performance Practice: Evolution of Performance and Pedagogy in the Viennese and English Schools." M.M. thesis, Bowling Green State University, 1976.

Discusses the relationship between the development of the instrument and the development of technique and pedagogy, inferred from C. P. E. Bach's *The True Art of Playing Keyboard Instruments*, Muzio Clementi's *Introduction to the Art of Playing the Piano Forte*, and J. N. Hummel's *A Complete Theoretical and Practical Course of Instructions on the Art of Playing the Piano Forte*. Bibliography. 45 pp.

165. Dudley, Raymond. "Harpsichord News." *Diapason* 60, no. 2 (January 1969): 10–11.

A brief history of the Viennese fortepiano. Also discusses the author's visit with Philip Belt, who specialized in building replicas of Viennese fortepianos. Photograph.

166. Klaus, Sabine K. "German Square Pianos with *Prellmechanik* in

Major American Museum Collections: Distinguishing Characteristics of Regional Schools in the Late Eighteenth and Early Nineteenth Centuries." *Journal of the American Musical Instrument
Society* 24 (1998): 27–80.

Examines instruments with *Prellmechanik* (an action type in
which the hammers are attached to the keys) housed in the De-
partment of Musical Instruments of the Metropolitan Museum of
Art (New York), the Division of Cultural History of the National
Museum of American History at the Smithsonian Institution
(Washington, D.C.), the Museum of Fine Arts (Boston), the Yale
University Collection of Musical Instruments, and America's
Shrine to Music Museum (Vermillion, S.D.). Discusses square pi-
ano building in Nuremberg and Augsburg, German influence on
American square pianos, and other background information. Pho-
tographs, illustrations.

167. Komlós, Katalin. *Fortepianos and Their Music: Germany, Austria, and England, 1760–1800.* Oxford Monographs on Music.
Oxford, England: Clarendon Press, 1995.

Discusses the piano and its music, performance, and performers during the second half of the eighteenth century. Part 1 is dedicated to the instrument, from Cristofori's invention to differences
between German/Viennese pianos and English pianos. Bibliography. 158 pp.

168. McGeary, Thomas. "Johann Lehmann's Fortepiano Tuning and
Maintenance Manual (1827)." *Early Keyboard Journal* 12 (1994):
71–94.

A translation of the entire *Gründliches vollständiges und
leichtfaßliches Stimmsystem* (1827) by Johann Traugott Lehmann.

169. ———. "Karl Lemme's Manual on Fortepiano and Clavichord
Maintenance (1802)." *Early Keyboard Journal* 8 (1990): 111–29.

A translation of Lemme's *Anweisung und Regeln zu einer
zweckmässigen Behandlung englischer und teutscher Pianoforte's
und Klaviere* (1802). The translator's introduction explains the
significance of the document, with a brief biography of Lemme.

170. "Music Trade Forum: Schroeter's Piano Action." *Musical Opinion* 87, no. 1041 (June 1964): 573.

A short article about the early piano actions and Schroeter's influence on the development.

171. "Music Trade Forum: The Evolution of Stringing." *Musical Opinion* 86, no. 1029 (June 1963): 573.

An essay about the stringing in early Viennese harpsichords and pianos upon examination of some surviving instruments.

172. Pollens, Stewart. "Early Nineteenth-Century German-Language Works on Piano Maintenance: A Review of Published Information Concerning the Stringing, Tuning, and Adjustment of the Fortepiano." *Early Keyboard Journal* 8 (1990): 91–109.

A review of six sources: *Stimmbuch oder vielmehr: Anweisung wie jeder liebhaber sein Clavierinstrument . . . selbst repariren und also auch stimmen könne* (1804) by Johann Heinrich Ernest Nachersberg; *Kurze Bemerkungen über das Spielen, Stimmen und Erhalten der Forte-piano, welche von Stein in Wien verfertiget werden* (1802); *Anweisung und Regeln zu einer zweckmässigen Behandlung englischer und teutscher Pianoforte's und Klaviere/nebst/einem Verzeichnisse der bei dem Verfässer verfertigen Sorten von Pianoforte's und Klavieren, von Karl Lemme, musikalischen Instrumentenmacher und Organisten in Braunschweig* (1802) by Karl Lemme; *Clavier-Stimmbuch oder Deutliche Anweisung wie jeder Musikfreund sein Clavier-Flugel, Forte-piano und Flugel-fortepiano selbst stimmen, repariren, und bestmöglichst gut erhalten konne* (1805) edited by Gall; *Ueber Klavierinstrumente, deren Ankauf, Behandlung und Stimmung* (1817) by Christian Friedrich Gottlieb Thon; and *Kurze Anleitung zu einer richtigen Kenntniss und Behandlung der Forte-pianos in Beziehung und Erhalten derselben, besonders derer, welche in der Werkstatte von Dieudonné und Schiedmayer in Stuttgart verfertigt werden* (1824). Discusses general construction, stringing, action regulation, tuning, voicing and tone, and miscellaneous repairs. The appendix is Thon's list of keyboard instrument makers.

173. Ritzenhein, Mark Steven. "Fortepiano Design and Construction."
     M.A. thesis, Michigan State University, 1990.

     In two sections. The first section is a study of design and
     construction of early Viennese pianos, principally through those of
     Johann Andreas Stein. Discusses acoustics and sound, case and
     frame, action, and performance practice. The second section dis-
     cusses the author's experience in building a replica of an early Vi-
     ennese instrument. The appendices include a chronological record
     of events related to the author's building of an instrument and a
     section on procedures for veneering and French polishing. Photo-
     graph, illustrations (many labeled). Bibliography. 182 pp.

174. Sumner, William L[eslie]. "Beethoven and the Pianoforte." *Music
     Teacher and Piano Student* 49, no. 8 (August 1970): 9–10; no. 9
     (September 1970): 17–18.

     Includes brief descriptions of Viennese pianos of Beethoven's
     time, and comments about the pianos at his disposal. Photographs,
     illustration.

175. Troeger, Richard. "Mozart's Piano and the Modern Grand."
     *Clavier* 30, no. 10 (December 1991): 18–23.

     A comparison of Viennese fortepiano of Mozart's time to the
     modern piano, from the performer's perspective. Photograph, il-
     lustrations.

## Canada

176. Kelly, Wayne. *Downright Upright: A History of the Canadian
     Piano Industry.* Toronto: Natural Heritage/Natural History, 1991.

     A history of the Canadian piano industry, from the late eight-
     eenth century to its decline in the early twentieth century. Also
     addresses dating and purchasing Canadian pianos, and organ
     builders. Includes an alphabetical list of Canadian manufacturers
     with brief descriptions and articles about prominent Canadian pi-
     anists. Photographs, illustrations, and facsimiles. Bibliography.
     160 pp.

# Czech Republic

Buchner, Alexander. *Musical Instruments through the Ages. See 47 under* History—General History.

# Denmark

177. Aanstad, Odd. "Some Examples for Piano Building in Norway and Denmark." In *Zur Geschichte des Hammerklaviers, Michaelsteiner Konferenzberichte, Band 50, 14. Musikinstrumentenbau-Symposium in Michaelstein am 12. und 13. November 1993*, edited by Monika Lustig, 135–142. Michaelstein/Blankenburg, Germany: Michaelstein Institut für Aufführungspraxis, 1996.

Discusses the history of early piano building in Norway and Denmark and contributions made by Norwegian and Danish piano makers. Mentions Andreas Marshall, Brödrene Hals, and Conrad Christian Hornung. Photographs.

# England

178. Clay, Reginald S. "The British Pianoforte Industry." *Journal of the Royal Society of Arts* 66, no. 3400 (January 18, 1918): 154–63.

A history of the British piano manufacturing industry. Includes an overview of the history of the piano.

179. Dahl, Bjarne, and John Barnes. "Changes in English Grand Piano Actions between 1787 and 1792." *Galpin Society Journal* no. 50 (March 1997): 208–11.

Discusses the development of the English grand piano action, inferred from the labels titled "Directions for Tuning and Keeping the Grand Piano Forte in Order" which were pasted on the back of the nameboards of Broadwood grands between 1787 and 1792. An actual label is reproduced in the article. Photograph, illustration.

Dahl, Christine. "Early Pianos and Performance Practice: Evolution of Performance and Pedagogy in the Viennese and English Schools." *See 164 under* History—Austria and Germany.

180. Kenyon de Pascual, B[eryl]. "English Square Pianos in Eighteenth-Century Madrid." *Music and Letters* 64, nos. 3–4 (July–October 1983): 212–17.

An article about the trading of English pianos in Madrid through examination of advertisement columns in newspapers.

Komlós, Katalin. *Fortepianos and Their Music: Germany, Austria, and England, 1760–1800. See 167 under* History—Austria and Germany.

181. Koster, John. "The Divided Bridge, Due Tension, and Rational Striking Point in Early English Grand Pianos." *Journal of the American Musical Instrument Society* 23 (1997): 5–55.

Examines the evolution of some piano design features in the eighteenth-century English pianos. Discusses bridge construction, scaling and timbre, strike points, and other developments. Evaluates related contemporary accounts and literature. Photographs, illustrations, graphs, tables, and facsimiles.

182. Maunder, Richard. "The Earliest English Piano?" *Galpin Society Journal* no. 42 (August 1989): 77–84.

Discusses a 1766 square piano by Johannes Zumpe, his earliest square piano and possibly the earliest English square piano. Addresses appearance, construction, and sound. Photographs; also see Plate VI (preceding p. 65).

183. Pleasants, Virginia. "The Early Piano in Britain (c. 1760–1800)." *Early Music* 13, no. 1 (February 1985): 39–44.

A history of early piano building in Britain. Photographs, facsimiles.

184. Rowland, David. "Piano Music and Keyboard Compass in the 1790s." *Early Music* 27, no. 2 (May 1999): 283–93.

Detailed article on the keyboard compass of British pianos of the period. Discusses Broadwood, Longman & Broderip, Southwell, and Clementi, and addresses the relationship between compass and piano works of the time. Photographs, illustrations.

185. Wilson, Chas West. "Instructions for Adjusting the English Piano Action." *Galpin Society Journal* no. 24 (July 1971): 105–6.

Discusses the instruction found on the label of a 1792 Broadwood grand piano. Includes the actual text, partially reconstructed by the author.

## France

186. Gil-Marchex, Henri. "Some Remarks on the Beginnings of the Piano in France." Translated by Rita Benton. *American Music Teacher* 12, no. 6 (July–August 1963): 24–25.

An article concerning the introduction of the piano into France in the late eighteenth century.

187. Koster, John. "Foreign Influences in Eighteenth-Century French Piano Making." *Early Keyboard Journal* 11 (1993): 7–38.

Discusses influences on French instruments by German and English piano builders, through Cristofori, Gottfried Silbermann, Johann Heinrich Silbermann (Gottfried's nephew), among others. The appendix contains a discussion about Claude Balbastre, a French composer of the time, and his association with the piano. Photographs, illustration.

## Italy

188. Rice, John A. "Stein's 'Favorite Instrument': A Vis-à-Vis Piano-Harpsichord in Naples." *Journal of the American Musical Instrument Society* 21 (1995): 30–64.

Discusses Norbert Hadrava's role in the dissemination of pianos (particularly Johann Andreas Stein's) in Italy and a piano-harpsichord he obtained for a nobleman in Naples. Describes a similar instrument now in Naples (dimensions, design and construction), possibly the same instrument obtained by Hadrava. The appendix contains excerpts from letters written by Hadrava about pianos and a *vis-à-vis* piano-harpsichord by Stein (in German and English). Photographs, facsimiles.

189. ———. "The Tuscan Piano in the 1780s: Some Builders, Composers and Performers." *Early Music* 21, no. 1 (February 1993): 5–27.

An article about the musical life in Tuscany as it pertained to the piano. The appendix contains articles (in both Italian and English) about Tuscan pianos by Giuseppi Zannetti, Francesco Spighi, Vincenzio Sodi, and Luigi Vignoli that appeared in *Gazzetta toscana*. Illustrations.

190. van der Meer, John Henry. "A Curious Instrument with a Five-Octave Compass." *Early Music* 14, no. 3 (August 1986): 397–400.

A description of a late eighteenth-century "tangent piano" exhibited at Museo Belliniano at Catania, Sicily. Photographs.

## The Netherlands

191. Gleich, Clemens von. *Pianofortes uit de Lage Landen* (Pianofortes from the Low Countries). Buren, The Netherlands: Haags Gemeentemuseum, 1980.

In Dutch and English. Published in cooperation with Frits Knuf BV. A collection of photographs and descriptions (including dates and measurements) of Dutch pianos in the collection at the Hague Municipal Museum. Includes a brief overview of the history of the piano in the Netherlands. Illustrations. Bibliography. 55 pp.

## New Zealand

192. Annabell, Angela. "A Colonial Pianoforte." *Early Music New Zealand* 3, no. 3 (September 1987): 24–26.

A general description and some background information on a square piano by Collard and Collard, brought to New Zealand in 1860 and currently housed in the Auckland Museum. Photograph, illustration.

## Norway

Aanstad, Odd. "Some Examples for Piano Building in Norway and Denmark." *See 177 under* History—Denmark.

## Poland

193. Vogel, Benjamin. "The Piano as a Symbol of Burgher Culture in Nineteenth-Century Warsaw." *Galpin Society Journal* no. 46 (March 1993): 137–46.

A social history of the piano in Warsaw in the nineteenth century. The appendix lists selected Polish piano makers in the nineteenth century. Photographs.

194. ———. "Two Tangent Square Pianos in Poland." *Journal of the American Musical Instrument Society* 20 (1994): 84–89.

Discusses the origins and constructions of two tangent square pianos from the last quarter of the eighteenth century, owned by the Muzeum Diecezjalne (Diocesan Museum) in Sandomierz and the Muzeum Narodowe (National Museum) in Cracow. Photograph, illustration (labeled).

## Portugal

195. Pollens, Stewart. "The Early Portuguese Piano." *Early Music* 13,

no. 1 (February 1985): 18–27.

A history of early Portuguese piano building. Technical discussions center around a Portuguese piano at the Lisbon Conservatory and another in a private collection by Harold Lester. Comparisons of Portuguese instruments to Cristofori's. Photographs, detailed illustrations.

## Spain

Kenyon de Pascual, B[eryl]. "English Square Pianos in Eighteenth-Century Madrid." *See 180 under* History—England.

196. Kenyon de Pascual, Beryl, and David Law. "Another Early Iberian Grand Piano." *Galpin Society Journal* no. 48 (March 1995): 68–93.

A detailed description of an anonymous Iberian piano restored by Arnold Dolmetsch as a harpsichord. The appendix contains information about key measurements and scaling of the instrument. Photographs, illustrations, graphs, tables. Bibliography.

## Sweden

197. Vogel, Benjamin. "Historic Keyboard Instruments of the Academic Orchestra in Lund." *Galpin Society Journal* no. 51 (July 1998): 154–69.

An overview of the thirteen keyboard instruments used by the orchestra from 1745 to 1850, including three pianos. Appendix 1 contains more detailed descriptions of three preserved historic keyboard instruments including a square piano. Appendix 2 contains information about the Swedish instrument makers mentioned in the article. Photographs, illustrations.

## United States

198. Arnold, Janice M. "American Pianos: Revolution and Triumph." *Clavier* 26, no. 6 (1987): 16–22.

   A history of American piano manufacturing and manufacturers. Photographs, illustrations.

199. Baltimore Museum of Art. *Musical Instruments and Their Portrayal in Art.* With a foreword by Adelyn D. Breeskin. Baltimore: Baltimore Museum of Art, 1946.

   Also see "Baltimore's Contribution to the Development of the Pianoforte" by Frederick Philip Stieff. Although much of the book is an iconography, the section on musical instruments contains descriptions of several early pianos at the museum (owned or on loan). 48 pp.

200. Dannemiller, Joanne Dilley. "The Development of the Importance of the Piano in America." M.A. thesis, Kent State University, 1959.

   A history of the piano from its introduction to America in the eighteenth century. Also discusses the effect of the piano on American music and musical life. While much of the book focuses on the literature and musicians, topics include the social history of the piano and the relationship of the piano to the American music industry. Bibliography. 84 pp.

201. Greenfield, Jack. *A History of Midwestern Piano Manufacturing.* Kansas City: Piano Technicians Foundation, 1996.

   Topics include builders and the industry, marketing and sales, labor relations, player pianos and their effect on the industry, pianos and entertainment, American Steel and Wire Meetings and their influence on the development of the piano, and the introduction of the spinet and console and its effect on the industry. Many manufacturers are discussed. Illustrations. Bibliography. 156 pp.

202. Groce, Nancy Jane. "Musical Instrument Making in New York City during the Eighteenth and Nineteenth Centuries." Ph.D. dis-

sertation, University of Michigan, 1982.

In two parts. Part 1 is a historical overview of musical instrument making in New York City before 1890, through a chronological study of the instrument makers including, but not limited to, piano builders. Part 2 is a biographical dictionary containing information about more than seven hundred builders and their shops or factories. Appendix 1 is an inventory at Steinway & Sons taken on May 1, 1856; appendix 2 contains papers of incorporation of the New York Piano-Forte Company; appendix 3 is an index of builders by instrument type. Illustrations. Bibliography. 552 pp.

203. Hume, Paul, and Ruth Hume. "The Great Chicago Piano War." *American Heritage* 21, no. 6 (October 1970): 16–21.

Addresses issues that surfaced during the World's Columbian Exposition concerning piano manufacturers, particularly the conflicts between piano manufacturers and the fiasco that resulted from the conflicts. Photographs.

204. Kirk, Elise K. *Musical Highlights from the White House*. Malabar, Fla.: Krieger Publishing Company, 1992.

Discusses the musical life at the White House from the time of George Washington to the time of George Bush. Based on the author's previous book, *Music at the White House: A History of the American Spirit* (Urbana: University of Illinois Press, 1986). Photographs, illustrations. Bibliographical essay. 242 pp.

205. ———. *Music at the White House: A History of the American Spirit*. Urbana: University of Illinois Press, 1986.

Discusses the musical life at the White House from the time of George Washington to the time of Ronald Reagan. Discusses pianos used at the White House, relationships between piano builders and the White House. See also *Musical Highlights from the White House* (Malabar, Fla.: Krieger Publishing Company, 1992), by the same author. Photographs, illustrations. Bibliographical essay. 457 pp.

206. Libin, Laurence [Elliot]. "A Unique German-American Square Piano." *Early Keyboard Journal* 9 (1991): 7–20.

Describes in detail a piano of unknown origin brought to Pennsylvania, presumably from Germany. Photographs.

207. Loest, Roland. "American Pianos: Evolution and Decline." *Clavier* 26, no. 6 (1987): 34–39.

An article about the history of American piano manufacturing through the 1980s. Photographs.

208. ———. "Square but Grand." *Piano Quarterly* 39, no. 153 (Spring 1991): 29–31.

About a mass burning of square pianos in Atlantic City in the early twentieth century.

209. Mann, Walter Edward. "Piano Making in Philadelphia before 1825." Ph.D. dissertation, University of Iowa, 1977.

Discusses the relationship between the cabinet making industry and the piano making industry, influences and differences from the piano technology outside the Philadelphia area, and piano builders. The appendix is an alphabetical list of piano builders and their surviving instruments from the pre-1825 Philadelphia area. Photographs, illustrations. Bibliography. 227 pp.

210. Moody, Dana M. "Keyboard Instrument Manufacturers and Casements in the Natchez, Mississippi Area (1850–1860): A Historic Study." M.S. thesis, University of Tennessee, Knoxville, 1995.

Examines the surviving historical pianos located in the area, regarding the pianos primarily as decorative art pieces. The thesis is concerned with piano ownership and trade in the area in the mid-nineteenth century rather than local piano manufacturing. Photographs. Bibliography. 132 pp.

211. Parton, James. "The Piano in the United States." *Atlantic Monthly* 20, no. 117 (July 1867): 82–98.

Topics include the history of piano making in the United States and abroad and the current (at the time of publication) state of manufacturing and trade.

212. *The Piano—A Mirror of American Life: The Schubert Club Keyboard Instrument Collection.* St. Paul, Minn.: The Schubert Club, 1981.

A collection of essays published on the occasion of a keyboard instrument exhibit by the Schubert Club (St. Paul, Minn.) in 1981. The essays include "The Domestic Piano in America" by Helen Rice Hollis, "The Piano and American Victorian Thought" by Clifford C. Clark, Jr., "'The Instrument of the Immortals' or 'Music for the Millions': The Manufacture and Sales of Pianos in America" by Emily Rosenberg, and "The Role of the Piano in the Lives of American Women in the Nineteenth and Early Twentieth Centuries" by Gretchen Kreuter. Includes a list of the instruments in the exhibit. Photographs, illustrations. 60 pp.

213. Roell, Craig H. "Confronting the Consumer Culture: The American Piano Industry, 1890–1940." Ph.D. dissertation, University of Texas at Austin, 1986.

A study of the piano as a reflection of American culture. Discusses merchandising, economy, and the business aspect of the piano industry. The appendices include a list of piano companies and products c. 1916, with location and production information, and an organizational chart for Baldwin Company c. 1916. Bibliography. 360 pp.

214. ———. *The Piano in America, 1890–1940.* Chapel Hill: University of North Carolina Press, 1989.

A history of piano and its industry in the United States. Discusses manufacturers, production and marketing, industry structure, and events and circumstances affecting the industry. The appendix includes the organizational structure of the Baldwin Company, a list of piano companies as of c. 1916 with their locations, dates of establishment, and production volumes, and a table of number of musicians and teachers of music from 1900 to 1940.

Photographs, illustrations. Bibliography. 396 pp.

215. Spillane, Daniel. *History of the American Pianoforte: Its Technical Development, and the Trade.* New York: by the author, 1890. Reprint, with an introduction by Rita Benton. New York: Da Capo Press, 1969.

A history of piano construction, manufacturing, and trade in the United States. Chapters are organized by cities. Includes a brief history of the keyboard instruments leading to the invention of the piano and of the early European piano making particularly in London. Appendix A lists prominent pianists and teachers; appendix B lists important patents from 1796 to 1890. Illustrations. 383 pp.

216. Stieff, Frederick Philip. "Baltimore's Contribution to the Development of the Pianoforte." In *Musical Instruments and Their Portrayal in Art,* by Baltimore Museum of Art, with a foreword by Adelyn D. Breeskin, 25–30. Baltimore: Baltimore Museum of Art, 1946.

A history of piano making in Baltimore and influences of Baltimoreans on the industry.

217. Young, Clarence E., ed. *Metropolitan Cincinnati.* Cincinnati: by the editor, 1927.

A description and a history of Cincinnati, with special attention to the industries. Includes a brief overview of the Wurlitzer Company (see pp. 16–17). A list of companies in Cincinnati titled "Index of Industrial Cincinnati" includes seven piano and player piano manufacturers. Illustrations.

# Builders and Manufacturers

## General

218. "American Pianos: Of Late Years Old Pianos Are Highly Prized as Antiques." *Antiquarian* 3, no. 3 (October 1924): 12–13.

Discusses piano makers and dealers up to the early nineteenth century. Photographs.

219. Anderson, Robert G., ed. *Dealer's Handbook of Pianos and Their Makers: Including Organs and Their Makers*. 1972 ed. Tulsa, Okla.: by the editor, 1972.

Alphabetical lists of manufacturers. An entry may contain addresses and phone numbers of the offices and factories, date of establishment, names of the current officers (as of publication), a list of divisions, subsidiaries, and other services, a list of brand names currently in production (as of publication), and a list of brand names owned but no longer produced. Includes an index of piano brand names. Organ manufacturers are organized in a separate list. 24 pp.

220. Boalch, Donald H. *Makers of the Harpsichord and Clavichord, 1440 to 1840*. 3rd ed. Edited by Charles Mould. Oxford, England: Clarendon Press, 1995.

Part 1 contains brief biographical sketches of the builders; part 2 contains description, dates, ownership, and notes about surviving early keyboard instruments (harpsichords and clavichords). While the main focus is on the harpsichord and clavichord, some information pertinent to the early piano is included. Geographical and chronological conspectus of builders, a list of London apprentices, index and translations of technical terms in seven languages, genealogies, and a bibliography. 788 pp.

221. Campbell, David Eugene. "The Purveyor as Patron: The Contribution of American Piano Manufacturers and Merchants to Musical Culture in the United States, 1851–1914." Ph.D. dissertation, City University of New York, 1984.

Examines the promotion of music by the American piano industry in the late eighteenth century to the early nineteenth century. Studies sponsorship of performances and contests, publishing, performances, building of concert halls and music schools, and other forms of patronage by the industry. The appendices contain tables used as evidence and reproductions of some primary sources. Illustrations. Bibliography. 544 pp.

222. Clinkscale, Martha Novak. *Makers of the Piano*. 2 vols. Oxford: Oxford University Press, 1993–99.

An alphabetical list of piano makers. Volume 1 covers years 1700–1820; volume 2 covers years 1820–1860. An entry may contain biographical information and descriptions of surviving instruments (dates, physical description, type of action, materials used in the construction, and former and current owners). Each volume has a bibliography, an annotated list of significant collections of pianos (public and private museums regardless of size of collection, private collections of at least five pianos), and a glossary. In addition, volume 2 contains illustrations of various piano actions in the appendix. 403 pp. (vol. 1), 487 pp. (vol. 2).

223. Flood, Grattan W. H. "Dublin Harpsichord and Pianoforte Makers of the Eighteenth Century." *Journal of the Royal Society of Antiquaries of Ireland* 39 (1909): 137–45.

While the article focuses on harpsichord making in eighteenth-century Ireland, it discusses piano builders such as Ferdinand Weber, his son Thomas Ferdinand Weber, and William Southwell

(Ferdinand Weber's apprentice), all of Dublin. Photographs, illustrations.

Golightly, John Wesley. "The Piano between 1800 and 1850: The Instruments for Which the Composers Wrote." *See 75 under* History—General History.

224. Groce, Nancy [Jane]. *Musical Instrument Makers of New York: A Directory of Eighteenth- and Nineteenth-Century Urban Craftsmen.* Annotated Reference Tools in Music, no. 4. Stuyvesant, N.Y.: Pendragon Press, 1991.

An alphabetical list of instrument makers in New York City during the eighteenth and nineteenth centuries, including piano builders. Each entry may contain information about dates, location, kinds of instruments made, and other relevant facts. Includes a list organized by instrument. Bibliography. 200 pp.

————. "Musical Instrument Making in New York City during the Eighteenth and Nineteenth Centuries." *See 202 under* History—United States.

225. Herzog, H[ans] K[urt], comp. *Europe Piano Atlas: Piano-Nummern.* 7th ed. Schriftenreihe Das Musikinstrument, Heft 2. Frankfurt am Main: Verlag Erwin Bochinsky, 1989.

In two parts. Part 1 contains serial numbers of "German, European, and Foreign" pianos (uprights, grands, harpsichords, and harmoniums up to 1988). Part 2 contains names of over fourteen hundred piano makers between 1600 and 1925, with their dates, locations, and other information, organized by country. In five languages (German, English, French, Swedish, and Italian). Glossary, bibliography. 159 pp.

226. Palmieri, Robert. "Artist and Artisan." *American Music Teacher* 12, no. 6 (July–August 1963): 26–27.

About early pianos and early piano builders such as Silbermann, Stein, Streicher, Graf, Pleyel, and Erard.

————. "300 Years of Piano History." *See 118 under* History—General History.

227. Pauer, E[rnst]. *A Dictionary of Pianists and Composers for the Pianoforte: With an Appendix of Manufacturers of the Instrument.* Novello, Ewer and Co.'s Music Primers and Educational Series, ed. John Stainer and C. Hubert H. Parry. London: Novello, Ewer and Co., [1895].

In two parts. The first part contains names and biographical information about performers and composers of the piano. The second part is dedicated to piano builders. A bibliography is included in the preface. 159 pp.

228. Pierce, Bob, ed. *Pierce Piano Atlas.* 10th ed. Albuquerque, N.Mex.: Larry E. Ashley, 1997.

Some previous editions are titled *Michel's Piano Atlas* or *Piano Atlas.* Contains locations and brief descriptions of manufacturers, piano names, serial numbers, and dates of manufacture. Photographs of some instruments. 448 pp.

Pollens, Stewart. "Early Nineteenth-Century German-Language Works on Piano Maintenance: A Review of Published Information Concerning the Stringing, Tuning, and Adjustment of the Fortepiano." *See 172 under* History—Austria and Germany.

229. *The Purchaser's Guide to the Music Industries.* New York: Music Trades.

Published annually since 1897 (title varies). Began as *The Piano and Organ Purchaser's Guide* by John C. Freund. Lists manufacturers in alphabetical order. Each entry may contain the name and location of the manufacturer with telephone and fax numbers, names of the officers, reviews of the instruments, and other background information. Also some background information on basic care and maintenance of the piano. May include separate lists of manufacturers and sellers of supplies, harpsichords, organs and chimes, sheet music, related books, music rolls/phonograph/radio, and other musical merchandise, as well as lists of retail music merchants, engravers and printers, finance companies, trade and other associations, and trademarks. Recent issues contain international sections.

230. Sadie, Stanley, ed. *The New Grove Dictionary of Music and Musicians*. 20 vols. London: Macmillan, 1980.

See under names of individual builders and manufacturers. An article may include discussions on topics such as the company history, biographical information, relevant inventions and products, brief descriptions of instruments made by the builder/manufacturer, and a bibliography.

231. Simon, Alicia. "Polish Instruments and Constructors of Instruments in Poland." In *Music Book*. Hinrichsen's Musical Year Book, edited by Max Hinrichsen, vol. 7, 220–26. London: Hinrichsen Edition, 1952.

Includes a section devoted to piano, including some unusual pianos made or conceived by Polish builders.

232. Taylor, S. K., ed. *The Musician's Piano Atlas*. Macclesfield, England: Omicron, 1981.

A list of piano builders and manufacturers, and the serial numbers by date. Useful in dating pianos. Full name of the company, location, and brand names for each entry. Includes "A History of the Piano from 1709 to 1980," by David S. Grover (photographs, labeled illustrations). The appendix, compiled by Bill Kibby, contains other miscellaneous pianos. See also *The Musician's Piano Atlas: Supplement No. 1* (Macclesfield, England: Omicron, 1984) by the same editor, which lists additional serial numbers and dates. 216 pp.

Wainwright, David. *The Piano Makers. See 149 under* History— General History.

233. Zuck, Barbara. "Step Aside Steinway, European Pianos in Finer Tune." *Columbus Dispatch*, 24 November 1985, sec. F, p. 4.

An essay comparing American Steinway pianos and German-made pianos.

## Allen, Mark

234. Levinson, Douglas. "Piano-Building Maverick Mark Allen." *Contemporary Keyboard* 5, no. 5 (May 1979): 16–18, 41.

About Mark Allen, a piano builder in Philadelphia, his pianos, and his business. Photographs.

## Allmendinger Piano & Organ Company

235. Wineberg, Susan. *The Allmendinger Piano & Organ Company: A Book Based on the Exhibit in the Lobby of the Allmendinger Building, South First Street, Ann Arbor, Michigan.* N.p., 1991.

Compiled by Jack Weiss. A booklet about the history of the company. Photographs. 16 pp. plus plates.

## Astin-Weight

236. Doerschuk, Bob. "New Piano Design: Innovation in Piano Design Survives among Craftsmen & Small Manufacturers." *Keyboard* 19, no. 12 (December 1993): 102–5, 107–11, 161, 176–77.

About Delwin Fandrich of the Fandrich Piano Company, Ray Astin of the Astin-Weight Piano Makers, and David C. Stanwood, and their respective inventions. Includes short interviews. Photographs.

## Babcock, Alpheus

237. Grafing, Keith G. "Alpheus Babcock: American Pianoforte Maker (1785–1842): His Life, Instruments, and Patents." D.M.A. thesis, University of Missouri, Kansas City, 1972.

An examination of thirteen of Babcock's surviving instruments and primary source documents about Babcock. Discusses his patents, especially the metal piano frame. The appendix includes photographs and general descriptions of the surviving instruments (such as appearance, materials used, and measurements). Illustrations (some labeled). Bibliography. 122 pp.

238. ————. "Alpheus Babcock's Cast-Iron Piano Frames." *Galpin Society Journal* no. 27 (April 1974): 118–24.

Discusses the controversy surrounding the invention of the cast-iron frame. Photograph opposite p. 128.

# Baldwin

239. *Baldwin: Today's Great Piano*. Chicago: R. R. Donnelley & Sons, Co., [1948].

A booklet intended for promotional purposes by the company. Includes lists of honors and awards, endorsements by artists, a brief history of the company, and an overview of the production process. Photographs, illustrations. 28 pp.

240. "Baldwin & Wurlitzer." *Music Trades* 143, no. 10 (November 1995): 76.

A short article about Rudolph Wurlitzer, Dwight Hamilton Baldwin, and the history of their respective piano manufacturing companies.

241. "Baldwin Granted Two Patents for Bass String Design." *Music Trades* 125, no. 11 (November 1977): 42.

One patent on the material design and wrapping of the bass string; the second on the special equipment required to produce the special bass strings.

242. "Baldwin's Period-Style Chickering Grands." *Music Trades* 146, no. 2 (March 1998): 156.

A short report describing three new Chickering model pianos and their features. Photograph.

243. Doerschuk, Bob. "Piano Builders Sound Off." *Keyboard* 14, no. 8 (August 1988): 38–40, 44, 46–50.

An article based on interviews with executives of Baldwin, Young Chang, Steinway, Yamaha, and Kawai. Topics include industry, trade, and production.

"A Grand Piano Is Born—A Story of Art and Industry." *See 80 under* History—General History.

244. Silverman, Robert J[oseph]. "A Report on a Great Piano Company: Baldwin." *Piano Quarterly* 32, no. 127 (Fall 1984): 60–62.

An essay about a tour of a Baldwin factory in Trumann, Arkansas, and an interview with factory manager Jimmy Smith during the tour. Photograph.

245. Wulsin, Lucien. *Dwight Hamilton Baldwin (1821–1899) and the Baldwin Piano.* With an introduction by John J. Emery. New York: Newcomen Society in North America, 1953.

An address given to the Newcomen Society in North America in Cincinnati on April 16, 1953. A biography and an early company history. Photograph. 33 pp.

## Bas, Louis

246. Koster, John. "Two Early French Grand Pianos." *Early Keyboard Journal* 12 (1994): 7–37.

Detailed descriptions of two surviving early French grand pianos, one made by Louis Bas (1781), the other made by Pascal Taskin (1787). Discusses inscriptions, dimensions, keyboard and action, stringing and scaling, other constructional features, and decoration. Compares the two instruments and discusses their significance. Photographs, illustrations.

## Baumann, Christian

247. Brauchli, Bernard. "Christian Baumann's Square Pianos and Mozart." *Galpin Society Journal* no. 45 (March 1992): 29–49.

Examines Baumann's life and his six surviving square pianos. Detailed descriptions of the pianos and their construction, including measurements. Also discusses the restoration process for the "Boston" piano. Photographs, illustrations, tables.

## Bechstein

248. Berkofsky, Martin. "A Bechstein Adventure." *Piano Quarterly* 34, no. 133 (Summer 1986): 22–24.

An essay based on a tour of the Bechstein factory in Berlin, Germany. Photographs.

249. *The House of Bechstein: Chronicle, 1853 up to the Present.* Berlin: C. Bechstein, n.d.

Text by Wolfgang Burde, design by Gabriele Burde. In English and French (English translation by Gisela Fricke). Topics include life and work of Carl Bechstein, the history of his piano manufacturing business, and his relationship with Hans von Bülow. Includes quotes about Bechstein instruments by noted musicians, past and present. Photographs, illustrations. 94 pp.

250. Reid, Graham. "European Pianos Analyzed." *Piano Quarterly* 35, no. 136 (Winter 1986–1987): 34–38; no. 137 (Spring 1987): 41–44.

Discusses Bösendorfer, Schimmel, Hamburg Steinway, Bechstein, Ibach, Grotrian-Steinweg, Blüthner, and Feurich.

## Beyer, Adam

251. Cole, Michael. "Adam Beyer, Pianoforte Maker." *Galpin Society*

*Journal* no. 48 (March 1995): 94–119.

Discusses Adam Beyer's innovations and the construction of his instruments. Includes a description of his 1779 square piano (no. 440). Photographs, illustrations.

## Blondel

252. "Recent Acquisitions: A Selection, 1991–1992." *Metropolitan Museum of Art Bulletin* 50, no. 2 (Fall 1992).

Includes an 1860 upright piano by Alphonse Blondel (see p. 41). Brief description and background information by Laurence Libin. Photograph.

## Blüthner

253. "Company Profile: Blüthner Piano Bids for U.S. Market— Competitively Priced Haessler Line of Uprights and Grands Will Be Unveiled at Winter NAMM." *Music Trades* 147, no. 1 (February 1999): 192, 195.

Discusses Blüthner's efforts to rebuild the company after the return of the business to the family, including the opening of a new factory and the introduction of the lower-priced Haessler pianos.

Reid, Graham. "European Pianos Analyzed." *See 250 under* Builders and Manufacturers—Bechstein.

## Boisselot

254. Stevenson, Robert. "Liszt in Andalusia." *Journal of the American Liszt Society* 26 (July–December 1989): 33–36.

Covers Liszt's concerts in Seville and Cádiz. Also discusses his Boisselot piano and Boisselot's two innovations (extra strings for sympathetic vibration, and a pedal similar to the sostenuto pedal).

## Bolin, Georg

255. "Swedish Piano." *Musical America* 84, no. 3 (March 1964): 13.

A short report on a piano with an adjustable soundboard, built by Georg Bolin.

## Bösendorfer

256. *Bösendorfer.* [Wiener Neustadt, Austria: Bösendorfer, 1978].

A commemorative booklet about the Bösendorfer firm and its pianos. Discusses history, development, and construction. Includes photographs of the instruments, and the manufacturing process. The appendix includes letters received by Bösendorfer from various artists. Illustrations, facsimiles. 44 pp., unpaginated (plus a folded page).

257. Doerschuk, Bob. "Boesendorfer: Celebrating 150 Years of Piano-Building Excellence." *Contemporary Keyboard* 5, no. 6 (June 1979): 8–14.

Discusses Ignaz Bösendorfer, the Bösendorfer pianos and the history of Bösendorfer's business. Photographs.

258. Fleming, Shirley. "Bösendorfer's Birthday Party—Under U.S. Ownership, an Old Firm Flourishes." *High Fidelity and Musical America* 28, no. 12 (December 1978): MA34–MA36.

A brief history of Bösendorfer piano firm and a short report on the firm's one-hundred-fiftieth anniversary celebration. Photographs.

Reid, Graham. "European Pianos Analyzed." *See 250 under* Builders and Manufacturers—Bechstein.

## Bradbury, William Batchelder

259. Wingard, Alan Burl. "The Life and Works of William Batchelder Bradbury 1816–1868." D.M.A. dissertation, Southern Baptist Theological Seminary, 1973.

While the dissertation focuses on Bradbury's contribution to church music, a section is devoted to his piano manufacturing business and instruments. The appendices discuss primary sources about Bradbury. Photographs. Bibliography. 575 pp.

## Brewer, Charles W.

260. Paulson, Christopher. "Organ and Piano Builder: Charles W. Brewer." *Focus on Racine County History* 15, no. 3 (Summer 1997): 1, 3.

Discusses the life and work of Charles W. Brewer. Partly based on an interview with Brewer in 1910. Includes a list of his patents. Photographs. Bibliography.

## Broadwood

261. Bilson, Malcolm. "A Tale of Two Pianos." *Keyboard Classics* 2, no. 4 (July–August 1982): 11–13.

A comparison of Stein pianos and Broadwood pianos. Discusses construction, sound, and their effect on performance of eighteenth-century music. Illustrations.

262. Burnett, Richard. "English Pianos at Finchcocks." *Early Music* 13, no. 1 (February 1985): 45–51.

An essay about the Broadwood and the Clementi pianos at Finchcocks. Includes brief backgrounds and descriptions of the instruments. Photographs.

Colt, C. F. "Early Pianos: Their History and Character." *See 53 under*

History—General History.

Dahl, Bjarne, and John Barnes. "Changes in English Grand Piano Actions between 1787 and 1792." *See 179 under* History—England.

263. Drake, Kenneth. "Behind the Fallboard." *American Music Teacher* 12, no. 6 (July–August 1963): 16–17.

A comparison of two pianos from Beethoven's time: an 1817 Broadwood and an 1816 Streicher. Discusses the actions, the damper systems, the strings, and the frame. Illustrations (labeled).

264. ———. "Broadwood Specifics." *Clavier* 15, no. 1 (January 1976): 22.

Brief descriptions of the 1806, 1818, and 1850 Broadwood pianos. Discusses action, compass, and pedals. Illustration.

265. Ludden, Bennet. "Beethoven's Broadwood: A Present-Day Memoir." *Juilliard Review* 8, no. 2 (Spring 1961): 9–11, 15.

Discusses an 1817 Broadwood grand piano owned by the author (a near replica of the Beethoven Broadwood), and its restoration. Photographs.

266. Melville, Derek. "Beethoven's Pianos." In *The Beethoven Reader*, ed. Denis Arnold and Nigel Fortune, 41–67. New York: W. W. Norton & Company, 1971.

Discusses construction of pianos associated with Beethoven and his personal relationship with piano builders. Includes Beethoven's letters to Johann Andreas Streicher, Nannette Streicher, Thomas Broadwood, Matthäus Andreas Stein. Photographs.

Rowland, David. "Piano Music and Keyboard Compass in the 1790s." *See 184 under* History—England.

267. Wainwright, David. *Broadwood by Appointment: A History.* With a foreword by Peter Smith. London: Quiller Press, 1982.

Discusses the history of the Broadwood family, the piano business, and the Broadwood instruments, from the birth of John Broadwood to the early 1980s. Includes a Broadwood family tree. The appendix includes technical information about Broadwood square pianos, grands, uprights, upright grands, cabinet pianos, strings, and the action. Photographs, illustrations. Bibliography. 360 pp.

268. ———. "John Broadwood, the Harpsichord and the Piano." *Musical Times* 123, no. 1676 (October 1982): 675–78.

An excerpt from his book, *Broadwood by Appointment: A History* (London: Quiller Press, 1982). Discusses Broadwood's contribution to the development of the piano and its effect on the harpsichord market. Photographs.

269. Warner, Robert A. "Two Early Square Pianos." *American Music Teacher* 12, no. 6 (July–August 1963): 21–23, 31.

Examines the square pianos by John Broadwood and by Sebastian Erard in the Stearns Collection of Musical Instruments at the University of Michigan. Includes physical descriptions, details of construction, and brief biographies of the builders. Photographs, illustrations.

Wilson, Chas West. "Instructions for Adjusting the English Piano Action." *See 185 under* History—England.

## Brodwin

270. "Brodwin Piano Co. Repairs 'the Siena Pianoforte.'" *Music Trade Review* 112, no. 10 (October 1953): 15.

A brief report about the Siena Pianoforte and Brodwin's restoration of the instrument. Photograph.

## Casteel

271. Pereira, L. A. Esteves. "A Forte-Piano at the Instrumental Museum—Lisbon." *English Harpsichord Magazine* 3, no. 4 (April 1983): 67–60.

A detailed description of a 1763 piano by Henrique van Casteel, a Flemish piano maker in Portugal. Discusses dimensions, the case and finish, stringing, keyboard, action, and the current condition of the instrument. Photographs.

## Chickering

272. *Achievement: An Ascending Scale, Being a Short History of the House of Chickering and Sons.* Boston: Chickering and Sons, 1920.

Discusses Jonas Chickering's life, the Chickering family, and the Chickering piano manufacturing business. Topics include the first instruments by Chickering, inventions, the factory, and the Chickering Hall in New York. Includes a list of endorsers of the instruments and a chronological list of important events in the history of Chickering and Sons. Photographs, illustrations. 28 pp., unpaginated.

273. *The Commemoration of the Founding of the House of Chickering & Sons upon the Eightieth Anniversary of the Event.* Boston: Chickering & Sons, 1904.

The commemoration exercises took place in 1903. Includes a short account of the commemoration, an address given at the commemoration, a short article about the life and work of Jonas Chickering, a history of the House of Chickering, and a brief history of the Chickering Halls in New York and Boston. Also includes a list of prominent musicians who played Chickering pianos and a record of a tribute to Jonas Chickering. Photographs, illustrations. 93 pp.

274. Gamet, Vera. "The Pianos of Jonas Chickering." *Old-Time New*

*England* 31, no. 1 (July 1940): 1–10.

Topics include his instruments, business, and his life. Photographs of Chickering pianos. Illustration.

275. Haupert, Mary Ellen Patnaude. "The Square Pianos of Jonas Chickering." Ph.D. dissertation, Washington University, 1989.

A study of Chickering's life and work, with particular attention to his square pianos. Examines twenty-four surviving square pianos by Chickering, discussing case and frame, action, and stringing. Detailed descriptions of the casings. A short glossary on p. 99. Appendix A contains transcriptions (with illustrations) of patent letters, two by Chickering and one by Alpheus Babcock. Appendix B contains tables of various string measurements, compasses, hammer and pedal characteristics, nameplate inscriptions, and case dimensions. Photographs, illustrations. Bibliography. 139 pp.

276. Hunt, Constance. "Chickering & Sons: Its Pianos, Its Commercial Enterprise, and Its Relationship to America's Musical Development." M.M. thesis, Florida State University, 1986.

A history of Chickering & Sons from 1823 to 1900 and its influence on musical development in America. Discusses the history of the piano in America, Jonas Chickering's background and training, and the firm's effects on the piano industry. Bibliography. 125 pp.

277. *The Jonas Chickering Centennial Celebration: A Tribute to the Life and Work of Jonas Chickering, One of the World's Greatest Inventors, in Celebration of the Hundredth Anniversary of the Founding by Him of the House of Chickering and Sons in 1823.* Boston: Chickering & Sons, 1924.

Contains a biographical sketch of Jonas Chickering, a brief history of the company, details of the centennial celebration (including programs, transcripts of the addresses given at the events, and tributes) and a short section about the New Chickering Hall in New York City. Photographs, illustrations. 55 pp.

278. Lott, R. Allen. "Chickering, Steinway, and Three Nineteenth-Century European Piano Virtuosos." *Journal of the American Musical Instrument Society* 21 (1995): 65–85.

Discusses the relationships between European pianists Sigismond Thalberg, Anton Rubinstein, and Hans von Bülow, and American piano firms Chickering and Steinway, during the nineteenth century. Illustrations.

279. Parker, Richard G[reen]. *Tribute to the Life and Character of Jonas Chickering: "By One Who Knew Him Well."* Boston: William P. Tewksbury, 1854.

Recollections about the life of Jonas Chickering, particularly about his character and relationships with others. The appendix contains newspaper articles about Chickering's death. Illustration. 162 pp.

280. Wignall, Harry James. "Chickering's 'Old Ironsides.'" *Piano Quarterly* 36, no. 142 (Summer 1988): 60–63.

Discusses the life and work of Jonas Chickering. Illustrations. Bibliography.

281. ———. "Father of the Modern Piano: The Legend of Jonas Chickering." *Keyboard Classics* 8, no. 3 (May–June 1988): 14–15.

Discusses the life of Jonas Chickering and his piano building business. Photographs, illustrations.

## Clark, Frederic Horace

282. Andres, Robert. "'Cherubim-Doctrine,' *Harmonie-Piano*, and Other Innovations of Frederic Horace Clark." D.M.A. thesis, University of Kansas, 1993.

Includes a discussion about the *Harmonie-Piano*, a large piano with two keyboards facing each other, invented by Clark. Photographs, illustrations. Bibliography. 68 pp., 22 leaves, unpaginated.

283. ———. "Frederic Horace Clark: A Forgotten Innovator." *Journal of the American Liszt Society* 27 (January–June 1990): 3–16.

A biography of Clark. Discusses his philosophies, his works and methods, and his *Harmonie-Piano*. Photograph.

## Clementi

Burnett, Richard. "English Pianos at Finchcocks." *See 262 under* Builders and Manufacturers—Broadwood.

284. ———. "Muzio Clementi: Pianist, Composer and Piano Maker." *Organ Yearbook* 23 (1992–1993): 97–107.

A conversation between the author and Martin Renshaw, recorded in March 1992. Photographs.

285. Colt, C. F. "From My Collection." *Clavier* 16, no. 3 (March 1977): 23–25.

Descriptions of a cabinet piano by Collard and Collard and of a cottage piano by Clementi from the author's collection. Photographs (also see inside cover of the issue).

286. Graue, Jerald Curtis. "Muzio Clementi and the Development of Pianoforte Music in Industrial England." Ph.D. dissertation, University of Illinois at Urbana-Champaign, 1971.

While the dissertation focuses on Clementi's musical style, it includes comments about his interest in piano manufacturing. Bibliography. 336 pp.

Rowland, David. "Piano Music and Keyboard Compass in the 1790s." *See 184 under* History—England.

## Collard and Collard

Annabell, Angela. "A Colonial Pianoforte." *See 192 under* History—New Zealand.

Colt, C. F. "From My Collection." *See 285 under* Builders and Manufacturers—Clementi.

## Crehore, Benjamin

287. Luxton, Denning D. *Vose Reminiscences: Benjamin Crehore,
Lewis Vose, James Whiting Vose.* Watertown, Mass.: Vose &
Sons Piano Company, [1923].

A brief history of Vose & Sons. Topics include the Vose
family history and the family's relationship with Benjamin Crehore and his business. Photographs, illustrations. 22 pp., unpaginated.

## Cristofori, Bartolomeo

288. Guy, Suzanne [W.], and Donna [M.] Lacy. *The Music Box: The
Story of Cristofori.* Lawrenceville, Va.: Brunswick, 1998.

An illustrated children's book about Cristofori's invention of
the piano. Includes illustrations of Cristofori's piano action and
the modern piano action. Bibliography. 30 pp., unpaginated.

Koster, John. "Foreign Influences in Eighteenth-Century French Piano
Making." *See 187 under* History—France.

289. O'Brien, Michael [Kent]. "Bartolomeo Cristofori at Court in Late
Medici Florence." Ph.D. dissertation, Catholic University of
America, 1994.

About Cristofori's relationship with the Medici court and its
effect on his work. Discusses musical and non-musical backgrounds, Cristofori's duties and positions, and the inventory of
musical instruments at the court. The appendices include information about sources, transcriptions, translations, and a chronology
of primary sources about Cristofori. Bibliography. 222 pp.

290. Pollens, Stewart. "The Pianos of Bartolomeo Cristofori." *Journal*

*of the American Musical Instrument Society* 10 (1984): 32–68.

A detailed discussion of the three surviving Cristofori pianos dating from the 1720s. Tables compare the dimensions of the instruments. The appendix contains inscriptions, diameters of the existing (but not original) strings, and the case dimensions of the pianos. Photographs, illustrations.

291. Sills, Mrs. J. E. "Three-Hundredth Anniversary of Cristofori." *Southwestern Musician* 20, no. 4 (December 1953): 9.

A short article about the events and circumstances that led to Cristofori's creation of the piano. Written on the occasion of the probable three-hundredth anniversary of Cristofori's birth.

# Currier

292. "Currier's Radical New SSP 'Plate-Less' Piano." *Music Trades* 129, no. 7 (July 25, 1981): 92–94.

Describes a new piano by Currier Piano Company, which features the Strataphonic String Panel, a support system that replaces both the traditional piano back and the cast-iron plate. Photographs.

# Davison and Redpath

293. Kuronen, Darcy J. "A Pianoforte by Davison and Redpath, London, 1789: Its Historical Position and Restoration Considerations." M.M. thesis, University of South Dakota, 1986.

A detailed study of the instrument at the Shrine to Music Museum in Vermillion, South Dakota. Topics include historical background (with a general history of the piano), the manufacturers, physical descriptions of the instrument, and construction. A chapter about potential restoration of the instrument is included. Photographs, illustrations. Bibliography. 59 pp.

## del Mela, Domenico

294. Pollens, Stewart. "An Upright Pianoforte by Domenico del Mela (1739)." *Galpin Society Journal* no. 45 (March 1992): 22–28.

A detailed description of the instrument, including measurements. Discusses appearance and construction. Photographs preceding p. 17 and following p. 32., illustrations, tables.

## Dolge, Alfred

295. "Alfred Dolge Piano Forte Materials." *Newsletter of the American Musical Instrument Society* 27, no. 2 (June 1998): 14–16.

Discusses Dolge's life and his company that manufactured felts, soundboards, and other general materials used in piano making. Illustration.

296. Franz, Eleanor. *Dolge*. Herkimer, N.Y.: Herkimer County Historical Society, 1980.

A biography of Alfred Dolge. Discusses his life, his businesses (including his piano manufacturing business), and his contribution to the community. Photographs, illustrations. 106 pp.

## Dolmetsch, Arnold

297. van Zuilenberg, Paul Loeb. "Cecil Rhodes's 'Spinet.'" *Galpin Society Journal* no. 26 (May 1973): 138–40.

About a piano designed by Sir Herbert Baker and made by Arnold Dolmetsch. A photograph of the instrument preceding p. 145, illustration.

## Erard

298. Brightwell, C[ecelia] L[ucy]. *Heroes of the Laboratory and the*

*Workshop.* New ed. London: Routledge, Warne, & Routledge, 1860.

Illustrated by John Absolon. The lives and careers of prominent innovators and people who had an impact on their industry. Includes a chapter on Sebastian Erard. 222 pp.

299. Frederick, Edmund Michael. "The Big Bang." *Piano Quarterly* 32, no. 126 (Summer 1984): 33.

Compares the sounds of an 1868 Streicher grand piano and an 1893 Erard grand piano, owned by the author, to that of the modern grand piano as represented by Steinway grands.

300. Kiraly, William, and Philippa Kiraly. "Sebastian Erard and the English Action Piano." *Piano Quarterly* 35, no. 137 (1987): 49–53.

Discusses Erard's career and his invention of the double escapement mechanism. Bibliography.

Palmieri, Robert. "Artist and Artisan." *See 226 under* Builders and Manufacturers—General.

Warner, Robert A. "Two Early Square Pianos." *See 269 under* Builders and Manufacturers—Broadwood.


# Everett

301. Brownson, James. "What's New in Musical Instruments." *Etude* 69, no. 7 (July 1951): 22, 56.

A short report about the new musical instrument models and accessories, including pianos by Everett, Gulbransen, and Wurlitzer. Photographs.

302. *100 Years (1883–1983): Everett Centennial Album.* Buena Park, Calif.: Everett Piano Company, 1983.

An illustrated/photographic history of the Everett Piano

Company and a company chronology. 31 pp.

## Falcone

303. Fine, Larry. "Santi Falcone: The Persistence of Small-Scale Piano Craftsmanship." *Keyboard* 15, no. 1 (January 1989): 28–29.

    A short article about Santi Falcone's life and his piano building business. Photograph.

304. "Recreating the Famed Mason & Hamlin Piano: How a Small Boston Factory Strives to Build One of the Most Celebrated Pianos in History." *Music Trades* 138, no. 10 (November 1990): 64–68.

    Discusses the history of Mason & Hamlin and the reintroduction of their pianos into the market in 1990 by a new company (formerly Falcone Piano Company). Photographs.

305. Rhodes, Lucien. "Piano Man." *Inc.* 9, no. 1 (January 1987): 52–56.

    About piano maker Santi Falcone's mission, his piano company, and its business dilemmas. A shorter version of this article has been reprinted in *College Musician* 1, no. 3 (Summer 1987): 32–34. Photographs.

## Fandrich

306. Bargreen, Melinda. "Taking Action: Seattleites' Revolutionary Invention Is Music to the Ears of Pianists." *Seattle Times*, 6 March 1989, sec. E, p. 2.

    A report on the newly-invented action for vertical pianos (Fandrich piano).

307. "Braving the Mature Piano Market: Fandrich Piano." *Music Trades* 139, no. 12 (January 1992): 58.

A short report on a new upright piano by Fandrich, Model U-122.

308. Cotter, Marianne. "New Respect for the Upright Piano." *Music Magazine* 13, no. 1 (February–March 1990): 6–7.

A short report on the new upright action design by Darrell Fandrich and Chris Trivelas.

Doerschuk, Robert L. "New Piano Design: Innovation in Piano Design Survives among Craftsmen & Small Manufacturers." *See 236 under* Builders and Manufacturers—Astin-Weight.

309. Tasciotti, Lou. "The Technician's View." *Piano Quarterly* 39, no. 156 (Winter 1991–1992): 60–63.

Discusses major differences in construction between vertical and grand pianos. Includes a brief review of the Fandrich piano.

310. ————. "The Technician's View." *Piano Quarterly* 39 [*sic*], no. 156 (Winter 1991–1992): 60–63.

Explains the construction of vertical pianos. Discusses advantages and limitations of the instrument compared to grands. Includes comments about the Fandrich uprights. [Note: incorrect volume number; should be 40.]

## Fazer

311. Karlson, Anu. "Affordable Quality: The Secret of Success for Finnish Pianos." *Finnish Music Quarterly* no. 1 (1988): 38–43.

Discusses two Finnish piano manufacturers, Hellas and Fazer; their histories, manufacturing processes, and instruments. Photographs.

## Fazioli

312. "World's Largest Piano Debuts at Carnegie Hall." *Music Trades*

136, no. 1 (January 1988): 53.

A short report on the 10'2" grand piano by an Italian piano manufacturer Fazioli. Includes a brief profile of the company.

## Feurich

Reid, Graham. "European Pianos Analyzed." *See 250 under* Builders and Manufacturers—Bechstein.

## Graf, Conrad

Palmieri, Robert. "Artist and Artisan." *See 226 under* Builders and Manufacturers—General.

313. Wythe, Deborah. "Conrad Graf (1782–1851): Imperial Royal Court Fortepiano Maker in Vienna." Ph.D. dissertation, New York University, 1990.

Topics include Graf's business, instruments, and relationships with composers and other musicians. Detailed examinations of the instruments (identification of the instruments, appearance and casework, internal construction, tone, significance, and other related information). Includes a chapter on pianos attributed to Graf. Appendix A contains transcriptions of primary source documents. Appendix B is a descriptive catalog of the instruments with photographs and detailed illustrations. Photographs, illustrations, tables. Bibliography. 664 pp.

314. ———. "The Pianos of Conrad Graf." *Early Music* 12, no. 4 (November 1984): 446–60.

A biography of Conrad Graf. Appendix 1 is a list of surviving pianos by Graf; appendix 2 contains detailed descriptions of the "Bonn" piano (owned by Beethoven) and the Op. 2616 piano (owned by Schumann and Brahms). Photographs, illustrations.

# Grotrian

Reid, Graham. "European Pianos Analyzed." *See 250 under* Builders and Manufacturers—Bechstein.

315. "World View: New Techniques Uphold Traditional Values at Grotrian." *Keyboard* 17, no. 3 (March 1991): 28–29.

A five-stop photographic tour of the Grotrian factory in Brunswick, Germany.

# Gulbransen

Brownson, James. "What's New in Musical Instruments." *See 301 under* Builders and Manufacturers—Everett.

316. "New Gulbransen Pinafore Piano Weighs only 130 lbs. and Can Be Carried in Automobile." *Music Trade Review* 114, no. 8 (August 1955): 21.

A short report about the Pinafore piano with a smaller compass. Photographs.

# Hals, Brödrene

Aanstad, Odd. "Some Examples for Piano Building in Norway and Denmark." *See 177 under* History—Denmark.

# Harrison, Michael

317. Gann, Kyle. "Shifting the Scales." *Village Voice* 35, no. 10 (March 6, 1990): 88.

Discusses Michael Harrison's "Harmonic Piano," a 24-pitch-per-octave acoustic piano that can be tuned in just intonation in two different keys.

# Haxby

Colt, C. F. "Early Pianos: Their History and Character." *See 53 under* History—General History.

# Heilmann

Colt, C. F. "Early Pianos: Their History and Character." *See 53 under* History—General History.

# Heintzman & Company

318. Ross, James Andrew. "'Ye Olde Firme' Heintzman & Company, Ltd., 1885–1930: A Case Study in Canadian Piano Manufacturing." M.A. thesis, University of Western Ontario, 1994.

Discusses manufacturing, marketing and retailing, and company history. Includes a short history of the Canadian piano industry. Appendices include a Heintzman family history, a company chronology, estimated annual production, estimated annual Canadian piano production for selected years, and estimated Canadian piano exports and imports for selected years. Bibliography. 94 pp.

# Hellas

Karlson, Anu. "Affordable Quality: The Secret of Success for Finnish Pianos." *See 311 under* Builders and Manufacturers—Fazer.

# Hornung, Conrad Christian

Aanstad, Odd. "Some Examples for Piano Building in Norway and Denmark." *See 177 under* History—Denmark.

319. Møller, Dorthe Falcon. "C. C. Hornung and the Single-Cast Iron

Frame: An Early Break-Through in the Danish Piano Industry."
Translated by Thomas Munck. *Galpin Society Journal* no. 37
(March 1984): 48–56.

An article about Danish piano maker Conrad Christian Hornung. Discusses his patent for single-cast iron frame, circumstances surrounding the patent, and the significance of his invention. Photographs preceding p. 45.

## Huber, John

320. Libin, Laurence [Elliot]. "John Huber Revisited." *Journal of the
American Musical Instrument Society* 20 (1994): 73–83.

Discusses John Huber, a German-American piano maker, and
his surviving pianos. Topics include the origins and construction
of the pianos. See also "John Huber's Piano in Context," *Journal
of the American Musical Instrument Society* 19 (1993): 5–37, by
the same author. Photographs.

321. ———. "John Huber's Pianos in Context." *Journal of the American Musical Instrument Society* 19 (1993): 5–37.

About John Huber, a German-American piano maker in
Northampton, Pennsylvania, and his instruments. Discusses the
origin, the history, and the construction of the three surviving pianos. Includes tables of approximate dimensions and string
lengths of his instruments. Also see "John Huber Revisited,"
*Journal of the American Musical Instrument Society* 20 (1994):
73–83, by the same author. Photographs, facsimiles. Bibliography.

## Ibach

Reid, Graham. "European Pianos Analyzed." *See 250 under* Builders
and Manufacturers—Bechstein.

# Kawai

Doerschuk, Bob. "Piano Builders Sound Off." *See 243 under* Builders and Manufacturers—Baldwin.

# Kimball

322. Bradley, Van Allen. *Music for the Millions: The Kimball Piano and Organ Story.* Chicago: Henry Regnery Company, 1957.

    A history of the Kimball company from the founding of the company by William Wallace Kimball in 1857. Photographs, illustrations.

323. "'Perma Crown Tone Board' of Plywood Adopted by Kimball after 12-Year Test." *Music Trade Review* 109, no. 5 (May 1950): 19.

    A report about the laminated soundboard used by Kimball. Briefly describes the research and the advantages of the soundboard.

# Klavins, David

324. "Bonn Technician Builds World's Biggest Piano." *Instrumentenbau-Zeitschrift—Musik-international* 42, no. 5 (May 1988): 71.

    A short article about the oversized piano that David Klavins was building at the time of the article. Discusses the dimensions and the idea behind the design of the instrument.

325. Carrington, Douglas R. "The Klavins Piano." *Organ* 70, no. 278 (Autumn 1991): 199–204.

    Discusses experimental oversized piano by David Klavins and the ideas behind the construction. A short paper by Kaikhosru Shapurji Sorabji (published on September 13, 1924), "Towards a New Piano," which discusses similar ideas, is reproduced in full.

326. "High Notes." *Musical Opinion* 114, no. 1364 (August 1991): 272–74.

   Includes a short paragraph about an oversized (four meters or 11⅓ feet high, and weighing two tons) piano designed by David Klavins.

## Krakauer Brothers

Bretzfelder, Maurice Krakauer. *The Story of the Piano. See 44 under* History—General History.

## Janko, Paul von

327. Mason, Merle H. "The Janko Keyboard." *Piano Quarterly* 22, no. 87 (Fall 1974): 7–10.

   An article about the Janko keyboard and its implications on music theory and performance. Illustration.

328. Rieder, Kathryn Sanders. "Experimental Keyboards: The Janko." *Clavier* 9, no. 5 (May–June 1970): 14–16.

   A description of a keyboard invented by Paul von Janko in Hungary. Photographs, illustration.

## Laurence and Nash

329. "High Notes." *Musical Opinion* 112, no. 1335 (March 1989): 78–82.

   Includes a short paragraph about use of cowbone as keyfacing material by Laurence and Nash Piano Company.

# Longman & Broderip

Rowland, David. "Piano Music and Keyboard Compass in the 1790s." *See 184 under* History—England.

# Marshall, Andreas

Aanstad, Odd. "Some Examples for Piano Building in Norway and Denmark." *See 177 under* History—Denmark.

# Mason & Hamlin

330. "Betting on the Premium Piano Market: In a Small Plant, a Revived Mason & Hamlin Focuses on Building a Limited Number of Musically Superb Pianos." *Music Trades* 145, no. 12 (January 1998): 160–62, 64.

A report on PianoDisc's acquisition of Mason & Hamlin. Discusses company history, current state of the company, and production processes. Photographs.

331. "Mason & Hamlin: New Vertical Piano Unveiled at NAMM." *Music Trades* 145, no. 7 (August 1997): 237.

A short report describing the features of Model 50 Professional Upright. Photograph.

"Recreating the Famed Mason & Hamlin Piano: How a Small Boston Factory Strives to Build One of the Most Celebrated Pianos in History." *See 304 under* Builders and Manufacturers—Falcone.

# Miessner, W. Otto

Miller, Samuel D. "W. Otto Miessner's Small Upright Piano: Its Invention, History, and Influence on the Piano Industry." *See 110 under* History—General History.

## Mirabal, Francisco Peréz

332. Kenyon de Pascual, Beryl. "Francisco Peréz Mirabal's Harpsichords and the Early Spanish Piano." *Early Music* 15, no. 4 (November 1987): 503–13.

An examination of Mirabal's harpsichords and two of the surviving early Spanish pianos. A comparison of the instruments, suggesting that Mirabal may have also built pianos around 1750 or earlier. Photographs.

## Moór, Emanuel

333. Shead, Herbert A. *The History of the Emanuel Moór Double Keyboard Piano.* With a foreword by A. Howard. [London]: Emanuel Moór Double Keyboard Piano Trust, 1978.

Distributed by Unwin Brothers (Old Woking, England). Discusses the construction and development of the instrument, reactions to the instrument (includes reprints of articles and letters), and musical considerations. Also includes a short biographical sketch of Emanuel Moór and an article by Moór. The appendices discuss repertoire, the instrument's implications on piano playing, and production volumes and include a list of patents, an article about other attempts to modify the piano, and a glossary. Photographs, illustrations (labeled). 310 pp.

334. ———. "The Emanuel Moor Double Keyboard Piano." *Music Teacher and Piano Student* 47, no. 12 (December 1968): 9, 29.

Includes discussions about the advantages of the double keyboard, descriptions of the instruments with the double keyboards, reactions to the instruments, and a short summary of Emanuel Moór's life. A photograph of a Bösendorfer Moór Concert Grand.

## New York Piano-Forte Company

Groce, Nancy Jane. "Musical Instrument Making in New York City during the Eighteenth and Nineteenth Centuries." *See 202 under* History—United States.

## Nunn and Fischer

335. Miller, Willis H. "The Biography of a Piano." *Minnesota History* 19, no. 3 (September 1938): 318–21.

A history of the piano made in 1839 and owned by the author. Includes background information on the manufacturer, Nunn and Fischer.

## Pfriemer

336. "Pfriemer's 113-Year Tradition of Piano Hammer Crafting: Carefully Blending African & Texas Wool to Create One of the Piano's Most Important Components." *Music Trades* 131, no. 12 (December 1983): 96–98.

Discusses the history of Pfriemer Piano Hammer Company and their hammer production process. Photographs.

## Pape

Colt, C. F. "Early Pianos: Their History and Character." *See 53 under* History—General History.

## Pleyel

337. *A Fragmentary History of the House of Pleyel.* N.p., 1927.

A booklet about Ignace Pleyel's life, piano making at Pleyel, the company's relationship to the development of the piano, the

Pleyel collection of documents and other items. Also discusses the factories and branches of the company (at the time of publication) and the Pleyel Hall. Contains quotes by various musicians about the Pleyel pianos and Pleyel Hall. Includes a concert program (October 18, 1927), list of patrons. Photographs, illustrations. 23 pp.

Palmieri, Robert. "Artist and Artisan." *See 226 under* Builders and Manufacturers—General.

338. Ripoll, Luis. *Chopin's Pianos: The Pleyel in Majorca.* Translated by Alan Sillitoe. Panarama Balear Series. Palma, Spain: Galerías Costa, 1958.

Discusses Chopin's relationship with Camille Pleyel (Ignace's son who took over the business upon Ignace's death) and Chopin's Pleyel pianos, particularly the Majorca piano. Photographs, illustrations. 16 pp.

# Renner

339. "Specialization in Piano-Making: Mechanisms, Hammers, Tools, Repairs and Restoring Work from Renner in Stuttgart." *Musik international—Instrumentenbau-Zeitschrift* 41, no. 12 (December 1987): 774–76.

Discusses Renner, manufacturer of piano actions and hammer heads, and its company history. Photographs.

# Samick

340. "Samick Debuts New Designer Console Pianos." *Music Trades* 133, no. 7 (July 1985): 117–18.

A report on the American Designer Console pianos. Discusses the features of the instruments.

## Sauter

341. "Sauter Piano Defies Design Conventions." *Music Trades* 146, no. 7 (August 1998): 68.

   A short report on the new Sauter pianos designed by Peter Maly, a German furniture designer. Photograph.

## Schimmel

342. "Parting Glance." *Piano & Keyboard* no. 192 (May–June 1998): 66.

   A brief article on limited-edition art pianos designed for Schimmel by Otmar Alt. Photographs.

Reid, Graham. "European Pianos Analyzed." *See 250 under* Builders and Manufacturers—Bechstein.

Schimmel, Nikolaus. *Piano Manufacturing—An Art and a Craft. See 137 under* History—General History.

## Schroeter

"Music Trade Forum: Schroeter's Piano Action." *See 170 under* History—Austria and Germany.

## Schulze Pollmann

343. "Schulze Pollman [*sic*] Pursues Premium Piano Market in U.S." *Music Trades* 146, no. 5 (June 1998): 116.

   A short article about Schulze Pollmann, an Italian piano manufacturing company, and its pianos. Photograph.

## Seiler

344. "Company Profile: Seiler Piano Celebrates 150th Year—Aside from Sheer Longevity, Seiler Remains One of the Few Piano Makers Still in Family Hands." *Music Trades* 147, no. 1 (February 1999): 168, 170.

   A summary of the company history and Seiler instruments. Photographs.

345. "Knuckle Under!" *Piano & Keyboard* no. 179 (March–April 1996): 15.

   A short report about Super Magnetic Repetition (SMR), magnetically assisted action in Seiler's Model 131 Concert Upright.

346. "Seiler Applies New Technologies to Grand Piano Construction." *Music Trades* 143, no. 1 (February 1995): 238.

   A short report about Seiler's new action, redesigned "Amplivox" scale, the "Membrator" soundboard system, and the system for adjusting soundboard height in grand pianos.

347. "Seiler Uprights: Patented New Action Offers Faster Speed of Repetition." *Music Trades* 144 (May 1996): 43–45.

   A brief article about Super Magnet Repetition (SMR), patented by Seiler to be installed in its upright pianos.

## Silbermann

Koster, John. "Foreign Influences in Eighteenth-Century French Piano Making." *See 187 under* History—France.

Palmieri, Robert. "Artist and Artisan." *See 226 under* Builders and Manufacturers—General.

348. Pollens, Stewart. "Gottfried Silbermann's Pianos." *Organ Yearbook* 17 (1986): 103–21.

A detailed examination of the three surviving pianos by Silbermann. Comparisons with Cristofori's pianos. Includes detailed measurements. Photographs, illustration, and facsimile.

## Southwell, William

Flood, Grattan W. H. "Dublin Harpsichord and Pianoforte Makers of the Eighteenth Century." *See 223 under* Builders and Manufacturers—General.

Rowland, David. "Piano Music and Keyboard Compass in the 1790s." *See 184 under* History—England.

## Stanwood, David

Doerschuk, Robert L. "New Piano Design: Innovation in Piano Design Survives among Craftsmen & Small Manufacturers." *See 236 under* Builders and Manufacturers—Astin-Weight.

## Stein

*Note: See under Streicher for Nannette Stein.*

Bilson, Malcolm. "A Tale of Two Pianos." *See 261 under* Builders and Manufacturers—Broadwood.

349. Latcham, Michael. "Mozart and the Pianos of Johann Andreas Stein." *Galpin Society Journal* no. 51 (July 1998): 114–53.

Examines Stein's instruments through his notes and surviving instruments. Addresses stops, issues in dating his pianos, the *vis-à-vis* instrument, stringing, and sound. Traces the development of Stein's pianos, dividing his work into three phases. Photographs, illustrations.

350. ———. "The Pianos of Johann Andreas Stein." In *Zur Geschichte*

*des Hammerklaviers, Michaelsteiner Konferenzberichte Band 50, 14. Musikinstrumentenbau-Symposium in Michaelstein am 12. und 13. November 1993*, edited by Monika Lustig, 15–49. Michaelstein/Blankenburg, Germany: Michaelstein Institut für Aufführungspraxis, 1996.

> Discusses Stein's life and instruments. Includes descriptions of his surviving instruments. Divides Stein's work into three phases, and discusses and contrasts the phases. Topics include dating Stein's instruments, general construction, stringing, and sound. Also discusses the *vis-à-vis* instrument in Verona. Photographs, illustrations, facsimiles.

Melville, Derek. "Beethoven's Pianos." *See 266 under* Builders and Manufacturers—Broadwood.

Palmieri, Robert. "Artist and Artisan." *See 226 under* Builders and Manufacturers—General.

Rice, John A. "Stein's 'Favorite Instrument': A Vis-à-Vis Piano-Harpsichord in Naples." *See 188 under* History—Italy.

Ritzenhein, Mark Steven. "Fortepiano Design and Construction." *See 173 under* History—Austria and Germany.

## Steinway

351. "Ain't It Grand: Steinway & Sons Celebrates 135 Years of Celestial Sound by Building Its 500,000th Classic Piano." *Life* 11, [no. 7] (June 1988): 99–103.

> Includes a brief company history and comments about the company. Photographs.

352. Bartholomew, Ralph I. *The Making of a Steinway*. [New York]: Steinway & Sons, 1929.

> Illustrated by Winold Reiss. A descriptive tour of the Steinway factory. 18 pp., unpaginated.

353. Chapin, Miles. *88 Keys: The Making of a Steinway Piano.* 1st ed. New York: Clarkson Potter Publishers, 1997.

Illustrated by Rodica Prato. About the Steinway piano and the history of the Steinway family. Topics include history of the piano, piano parts, materials used, the acoustics of the piano, the assembly, and voicing. Includes a chronology of the instrument and significant events, both musical and non-musical. The appendix contains sales and contact information. Glossary/index. Photographs. 143 pp.

Doerschuk, Bob. "Piano Builders Sound Off." *See 243 under* Builders and Manufacturers—Baldwin.

354. ———. "Steinway: *Keyboard* Examines Rumors of a Piano Giant's Decline." *Keyboard* 19, no. 12 (December 1993): 86–98.

Discusses the corporate history of Steinway & Sons and changes that took place with the CBS acquisition.

355. Fostle, Donald W. *The Steinway Saga: An American Dynasty.* New York: Scribner, 1995.

A detailed history of the Steinway family and Steinway & Sons Company, from Henry E. Steinway's childhood in the early nineteenth century through the present. Illustrations. Bibliography. 710 pp.

Frederick, Edmund Michael. "The Big Bang." *See 299 under* Builders and Manufacturers—Erard.

356. Geczy, Charles K. "Contribution by Steinway Family Members to the Technical and Acoustical Capabilities of the Steinway Grand Piano." Ph.D. dissertation, New York University, 1989.

Covers some key Steinway family members and their contributions to the development of the company and the instruments. Discusses Henry Engelhard, Theodore, William, Henry (the third son of Henry Engelhard), Charles, and Albert Steinway in detail. Topics include labor relations, inventions and patents, and public and business relations. Includes introductory discussions about the history of the piano, construction and acoustics, and the manufacturing industry. Descriptions of Steinway grand models. Photographs, illustrations. Bibliography. 289 pp.

357. Goldenberg, Susan. *Steinway from Glory to Controversy: The Family, the Business, the Piano*. Oakville, Ontario: Mosaic Press, 1996.

Based on the interviews conducted by the author with Steinway family members, family friends, and others associated with the family or the business. Discusses important members of the Steinway family, their influence on the business, and the history of Steinway & Sons, including the years after the CBS acquisition. The family tree (includes only the members discussed in the history). Photographs, illustrations. Bibliography. 253 pp.

358. Grossman, John. "Grand Pianos." *Horizon* 25, no. 2 (March 1982): 50–57.

A tour of Steinway & Sons factory. Photographs.

359. Hoover, Cynthia Adams. "The Great Piano War of the 1870s." In *A Celebration of American Music: Words and Music in Honor of H. Wiley Hitchcock*, edited by Richard Crawford, R. Allen Lott, and Carol J. Oja, 132–53. Ann Arbor: University of Michigan Press, 1990.

Discusses the feud between Steinway and Albert Weber piano companies in the late nineteenth century. Illustrations. Bibliography.

360. ———. "The Steinways and Their Pianos in the Nineteenth Century." *Journal of the American Musical Instrument Society* 7 (1981): 47–89.

Discusses contributions by the Steinways to piano construction, the industry, and the success of the company in the nineteenth century. Photographs, illustrations.

361. Kammerer, Rafael. "The Steinway Dynasty: The Story of the Modern Piano." *Musical America* 81, no. 6 (June 1961): 6–9, 56.

Discusses Steinway & Sons Company and the Steinway family. Photographs, illustrations.

362. Lenehan, Michael. "The Quality of the Instrument." *Atlantic Monthly* 250, no. 2 (August 1982): 32–58.

A tour of the Steinway factory. Includes a history of Steinway & Sons.

363. Levine, Jo Ann. "Battle of the Concert Grands." *Christian Science Monitor* 70 (December 13, 1977): 14–15.

Addresses endorsement of pianos by professional pianists and criticism of Steinway since the CBS acquisition.

364. Lieberman, Richard K. *Steinway & Sons.* New Haven, Conn.: Yale University Press, 1995.

A history of the Steinway family and its piano business, from Heinrich Steinweg's childhood to the years following the sale of the company to CBS. Topics include family relations, social history, marketing, worker relations, and business dealings. A selective family tree. Photographs, illustrations. 374 pp.

Lott, R. Allen. "Chickering, Steinway, and Three Nineteenth-Century European Piano Virtuosos." *See 278 under* Builders and Manufacturers—Chickering.

365. Merkur, Rheinischer. "There's Nothing Quite as Grand as a Steinway." *German Tribune* no. 1287 (August 23, 1987): 10–11.

Discusses the Steinway family history and the history of Steinway companies in New York and Hamburg. Photographs.

366. Paderewski, I[gnace] J[an]. *Steinway Progress: An Appreciation.* New York: Steinway & Sons, 1927.

A facsimile along with a transcription of a handwritten letter by Paderewski to Steinway & Sons praising the company and their pianos. The letter is dated May 4, 1914. 5 pp., unpaginated.

367. Ratcliffe, Ronald V. *Steinway & Sons*. With a foreword by Henry Z. Steinway. San Francisco: Chronicle Books, 1989.

Discusses the family history up to the 1970s, the history of the company up to the CBS acquisition in the mid 1980s, the relationship between the company and musicians, and Steinway instruments. A section is devoted to art-case pianos by Steinway. Appendices include a list of patents by Steinway and a list of Steinway artists. Photographs, illustrations, facsimiles. Bibliography. 204 pp.

Reid, Graham. "European Pianos Analyzed." *See 250 under* Builders and Manufacturers—Bechstein.

368. Richards, Denby. "Steinway: Denby Richards Has Been Looking at Steinway's Plans for the New Millennium." *Musical Opinion* 118 [*sic*], no. 1406 (Summer 1996): 79–80.

An essay including a brief history of the Steinway piano manufacturing business (New York and Hamburg) and comments about the company. Photographs. [Note: incorrect volume number; should be 119.]

369. Rothstein, Edward. "At Steinway, It's All Craft." *New York Times*, 22 February 1981, sec. 4, p. 8E.

A short article about Steinway & Sons. Includes a brief history of the company and its piano making.

370. *Royal Appointments and Decorations Conferred in Appreciation of the Steinway Piano*. 2nd ed. New York: Steinway and Sons, 1912.

Descriptions of honors and awards received by Steinway & Sons. In three parts. The first part contains royal appointments; the second part is the description of the piano given to the White House in 1903; the third part contains decorations. Photographs, illustrations. 68 pp., unpaginated.

371. Rubinsky, Jane. "Business as Usual—for 138 Years: Steinway & Sons Builds Pianos the Old Fashioned Way." *Keyboard Classics*

11, no. 6 (November–December 1991): 6–7.

Discusses the piano building process at Steinway & Sons. Photographs.

372. Savard, David M. "88+34 Years above the Piano Stool: The Steinway Grand Action, 1979." TMs (Photocopy). Duke University Library, Durham, N.C.

Discusses the development of the Steinway grand action. Topics include mechanisms, improvements, and patents. The appendix contains illustrations and patent letters in chronological order. Bibliography (handwritten). 80 leaves.

373. Silverman, Robert Joseph. "A Talk with John Steinway." *Piano Quarterly* 30, no. 116 (Winter 1981–1982): 15–21.

An interview with John Steinway during a tour of the Steinway factory.

374. Steinway, John H. "The Piano: Tradition or Progress?" *Music Journal Annual—Anthology* (1963): 40.

A short essay about Steinway's history and current state of piano making.

375. Steinway, Theodore E. *People and Pianos: A Century of Service to Music.* New York: Steinway & Sons, 1953.

Published for the one-hundredth anniversary of the founding of the House of Steinway. The history of the Steinway family, the Steinway & Sons company, and the instruments, primarily through photographs and illustrations. 122 pp.

376. "The Steinway Traditional K-52: 'An Old Friend Returns.'" *Musik international—Instrumentenbau-Zeitschrift* 36, no. 2 (February 1982): 154–55.

Describes the features of the model introduced in 1981. Illustrations.

377. "Steinway's Landmark 500,000th Piano: Unique Case Design

Reflects an Inspired 135 Year Legacy." *Music Trades* 136, no. 10 (October 1988): 64–72.

An article about the history of the piano and Steinway & Sons, commemorating the production of the 500,000th piano by the company. Photographs, illustrations.

378. "The Talk of the Town: Change of Keys." *New Yorker* 33, no. 49 (January 25, 1958): 25–27.

Discusses Steinway & Son's switch from ivory to plastic key covering and the search for other substitute materials for ivory.

379. "Upbeats: Million Dollar Steinway Sold." *Piano & Keyboard* no. 191 (March–April 1998): 12.

A brief article about the 1884 art-case Steinway piano, auctioned at Christie's in London, with a description of the case design. Photograph.

380. "World View: Steinway Explores Ivory Substitute." *Keyboard* 19, no. 11 (November 1993): 14–15.

A short report about Steinway's joint research project with the Rensselaer Polytechnic Institute to develop synthetic ivory (RPIvory).

Zuck, Barbara. "Step Aside Steinway, European Pianos in Finer Tune." *See 233 under* Builders and Manufacturers—General.

## Story & Clark

381. Tittle, Martin B. "How Grand Pianos Are Made." *Clavier* 19, no. 5 (May–June 1980): 32–35.

A photographic essay about piano manufacturing. Photographs taken at the Story & Clark Piano Company. Descriptive captions.

## Strauch Brothers

Strauch Brothers. *The Manufacture of Pianoforte Action: Its Rise and Development. See 146 under* History—General History.

## Streicher

382. de Silva, Preethi. "Notes on an Early Nineteenth-Century Manual for Fortepiano Owners by Andreas Streicher, with an Essay Celebrating the One-Hundred-Fiftieth Anniversary of the Deaths of Nanette [*sic*] and Andreas Streicher." *Courant* 1, no. 3 (August 1983): 21–26.

In two parts. The first part of this article contains some introductory comments on Andreas Streicher's booklet, *Brief Remarks on the Playing, Tuning and Care of Fortepianos Made by Nannette Streicher née Stein in Vienna* (1801). The second part is a short biography of the Streichers.

Drake, Kenneth. "Behind the Fallboard." *See 263 under* Builders and Manufacturers—Broadwood.

Frederick, Edmund Michael. "The Big Bang." *See 299 under* Builders and Manufacturers—Erard.

383. Fuller, Richard A. "Andreas Streicher's Notes on the Fortepiano, Chapter 2: 'On Tone.'" *Early Music* 12, no. 4 (November 1984): 461–70.

A reproduction and a translation of Chapter 2 from Streicher's *Kurze Bemerkungen über das Spielen, Stimmen und Erhalten der Fortepiano*. Includes introductory comments. Facsimiles, photograph.

384. Keeling, Geraldine. "Liszt and J. B. Streicher, a Viennese Piano Maker." *Studia Musicologica* 28, nos. 1–4 (1986): 35–46.

Discusses Liszt's relationship with Johann Baptist Streicher and Liszt's use of Streicher pianos. Photographs.

Melville, Derek. "Beethoven's Pianos." *See 266 under* Builders and Manufacturers—Broadwood.

Palmieri, Robert. "Artist and Artisan." *See 226 under* Builders and Manufacturers—General.

385. Streicher, Andreas. *Brief Remarks on the Playing, Tuning, and Care of Fortepianos Made in Vienna by Nannette Streicher née Stein: Prepared Exclusively for the Owners of These Instruments.* Translated and with an introduction by Preethi de Silva. With a foreword by Malcolm Bilson. Historical Treatises on Musical Instruments, vol. 1. Ann Arbor, Mich.: Early Music Facsimiles, [1983].

Originally published in German in 1801. Chapter 3 is devoted to tuning, with general tuning instructions (including tuning hammer technique); chapter 4 discusses general maintenance and care of the piano (including climate issues and cleaning). The appendix is a translated excerpt from a letter written by Andreas Streicher to Dr. Carl Bursy. Illustration. 17 pp.


## Taskin, Pascal

Koster, John. "Two Early French Grand Pianos." *See 246 under* Builders and Manufacturers—Bas, Louis.


## Taws, Charles

386. Taws, Edward Town, and Mrs. Edward Town Taws (Helen May Talley). *Charles Taws, ca. 1743–1836, Musical Instrument Maker: His Career, His Progeny, and Some of His Descendants.* Edited by Grace Gale Paris. Philadelphia: by the authors, 1986.

A history and genealogy of the Taws family, starting with Charles Taws. The first three sections are about the life and work of Charles Taws, a Philadelphia piano and organ builder from the late eighteenth century to the early nineteenth century. Includes a list of his surviving pianos with their current locations and a photograph of a family piano built by Charles Taws. The remainder of the work discusses the genealogy of the family. 45 pp.


## Tonk, William

387. Tonk, William. *Memoirs of a Manufacturer*. With an introduction by C. A. Daniell. New York: Presto Publishing Co., 1926.

An autobiography. Includes background information about the Chicago area and the music industry, personal remarks about people and piano companies he knew, and miscellaneous anecdotes. Photographs, illustrations. 310 pp.


## Trivelas, Chris

Cotter, Marianne. "New Respect for the Upright Piano." *See 308 under* Builders and Manufacturers—Fandrich.


## Vose & Sons

Luxton, Denning D. *Vose Reminiscences: Benjamin Crehore, Lewis Vose, James Whiting Vose*. *See 287 under* Builders and Manufacturers—Crehore, Benjamin.


## Walter

388. Latcham, Michael. "Mozart and the Pianos of Gabriel Anton Walter." *Early Music* 25, no. 3 (1997): 382–400.

Examines Walter pianos, including unsigned or altered pianos, and a Mozart piano attributed to Anton Walter. Photographs, illustrations.

389. Rice, John A. "Anton Walter, Instrument Maker to Leopold II."

*Journal of the American Musical Instrument Society* 15 (1989): 32–51.

Discusses Anton Walter, a Viennese piano maker in the late eighteenth and early nineteenth centuries. Includes new information from three documents published for the first time. The appendix contains the documents (two letters and a decree) in facsimile, in the original German transcription, and in English translation.

## Weber (Ireland)

Flood, Grattan W. H. "Dublin Harpsichord and Pianoforte Makers of the Eighteenth Century." *See 223 under* Builders and Manufacturers—General.

## Weber (United States)

Hoover, Cynthia Adams. "The Great Piano War of the 1870s." *See 359 under* Builders and Manufacturers—Steinway.

## Wing & Son

*The Book of Complete Information about Pianos. See 43 under* History—General History.

## Wurlitzer

"Baldwin & Wurlitzer." *See 240 under* Builders and Manufacturers—Baldwin.

Brownson, James. "What's New in Musical Instruments." *See 301 under* Builders and Manufacturers—Everett.

390. "New Piano Soundboard Unveiled by Wurlitzer at NAMM-West." *Music Trades* 126, no. 2 (February 1978): 79–81.

A report on Wurlitzer's new soundboard in which three layers of spruce are bonded at specified angles.

391. Silverman, Robert J[oseph]. "A Talk with Executives of the Wurlitzer Corporation." *Piano Quarterly* 31, no. 123 (Fall 1983): 43–45.

An excerpt from an interview with Wurlitzer officials before the author toured the factory in Holly Springs, Mississippi.

Young, Clarence E., ed. *Metropolitan Cincinnati. See 217 under* History—United States.

392. Wurlitzer Company. *The House of Wurlitzer: 1856–1906.* [Englewood, N.J.]: Music Trades, 1906.

A brief history of the Wurlitzer Company. Also includes a short biography of Rudolph Wurlitzer. Illustrations. Reprinted from *Music Trades*, December 1, 1906, pp. 61–68. 8 pp.

393. "Wurlitzer's '2780' Pianos to Debut in New Orleans." *Music Trades* 133, no. 6 (June 1985): 50–52.

Discusses the new console series by Wurlitzer.

## Yamaha

Doerschuk, Bob. "Piano Builders Sound Off." *See 243 under* Builders and Manufacturers—Baldwin.

394. Stokes, Henry Scott. "On Yamaha's Assembly Line." *New York Times*, 22 February 1981, sec. 4, p. 8E.

A short article about Yamaha's piano making, particularly about automation. Photograph.

Yamaha International Corporation (Nippon Gakki Seizo Kabushiki Kaisha). *All about Yamaha Piano. See 156 under* History—General History.

395. "Yamaha Introduces Six New Everett Pianos." *Music Trades* 136, no. 10 (October 1988): 94–95.

Describes Yamaha's new line of Everett console and studio pianos. Photograph.

396. "Yamaha Pianos: Acoustic Baby Grand Added to Silent Series." *Music Trades* 143, no. 4 (May 1995): 126–27.

A short report on Yamaha's new baby grand piano A1S, the silencing mechanism, and other features available on the piano. Photograph.

## Young Chang

Doerschuk, Bob. "Piano Builders Sound Off." *See 243 under* Builders and Manufacturers—Baldwin.

397. "New Young Chang Soundboards." *Music Trades* 140, no. 3 (April 1992): 99.

A short column about the new soundboard design with asymmetrical crown and other developments in Young Chang pianos.

398. "Young Chang's G-208 Grand Piano Features All-New Scale." *Music Trades* 140, no. 12 (January 1993): 172–73.

Describes a redesigned grand piano by Young Chang, with a new soundboard design, a new scale design, and other new features.

## Zumpe

Maunder, Richard. "The Earliest English Piano?" *See 182 under* History—England.

# Construction and Design

## General Construction

399. Beasley, William Howard. "Let's Build a Piano." *Music Journal* 18, no. 5 (June–July 1960): 36–37, 53–54.

    An introduction to the basic construction of the modern piano. Illustrations.

400. Bezdechi, Adrian. *Pianos & Player Pianos: An Informative Guide for Owners and Prospective Buyers.* Portland, Ore.: Player Piano House, 1979.

    An introduction to the construction, maintenance, and care of the piano and the player piano. Discusses parts of the piano, purchase and selection, repairs, maintenance, and tuning. Appendix 1 discusses the Vorsetzer. Appendix 2 addresses the care and maintenance of piano rolls. Appendix 3 addresses refinishing pianos. Photographs, illustrations (labeled). 63 pp.

401. Bielefeldt, Catherine. *The Wonders of the Piano: The Anatomy of the Instrument.* Edited by Alfred R. Weil. With a foreword by Peter M. Perez. Melville, N.Y.: Belwin Mills, 1984.

    A photographic essay about piano construction. Discusses the history of the instrument, the mechanisms, materials, parts of the piano, and maintenance. Includes a chronology of important events in the history of the piano. Illustrations (labeled). Bibliography. 128 pp.

*The Book of Complete Information about Pianos. See 43 under* History—General History.

402. Challis, John. "New: A 20th Century Piano." *American Music Teacher* 12, no. 6 (July–August 1963): 20.

A short article about the attempts to build pianos with sounds of the early pianos but with twentieth-century construction.

403. Cooke, John. "Plank Expression." *Early Music Today* 7, no. 1 (February–March 1999): 5–7.

A description of the fortepiano construction process, with special attention to the selection of wood and its role in construction of the instrument. Photographs.

404. Cosgrove, Robert C. "Make Mine Music." *Music News* 42, no. 2 (February 1950): 7.

Discusses the differences between grand pianos, spinets, and studio uprights. Also addresses electric organs. Intended primarily for beginners. Photographs.

405. Donington, Robert. *The Instruments of Music.* 3rd rev. ed. London: Methuen & Co., 1962.

First published in 1949. An introduction to the construction of musical instruments. Includes a chapter on stringed keyboard instruments (harpsichord, clavichord, and piano). The appendices contain a glossary, a bibliography, and articles on tuning and temperament. Photographs (none of a piano), illustrations. 202 pp.

406. Drake, Kenneth. "Building a Mozart Piano." *Clavier* 5, no. 6 (November 1966): 23–25.

A report on the author's experience building a "Mozart-type" piano. Focuses on the action and the stringing. Photograph, illustrations (labeled).

407. Esterowitz, M[ichael]. "Piano Doctor." *Keyboard Classics* 2, no. 5 (September–October 1982): 14.

Discusses the basic construction of the piano and its main components (soundboard, plate, string, keyboard, and action).

408. Fine, Larry. *The Piano Book: Buying & Owning a New or Used Piano*. 3rd ed. With a foreword by Keith Jarrett. Boston: Brookside Press, 1994.

Illustrated by Douglas R. Gilbert. Topics include general maintenance, construction, moving, and purchase of the piano. Chapter 1: the action of the grand and the upright piano. Chapters 2 through 5: purchasing a piano, addressing considerations for purchase, new pianos (including digital pianos, accessories, and reviews by brands), and used pianos. Chapter 6: moving and storing a piano (both in-house and long-distance). Chapter 7: an overview of piano maintenance. Annual supplement published each August. Illustrations (many detailed and labeled). Glossary. 194 pp.

409. Fischer, J[erry] Cree. *Piano Tuning: A Simple and Accurate Method for Amateurs*. New York: Dover Publications, 1975.

Originally published under the title *Piano Tuning, Regulating and Repairing: A Complete Course of Self Instruction in the Tuning of Pianos and Organs*. A textbook on history, construction, maintenance and repair, and tuning and temperament. Also includes a section on organ tuning, maintenance and repair. The original publication (Philadelphia: Theodore Presser, 1907) contained additional sections ("Practical Application of Piano Tuning as a Profession," "Business Hints," "Ideas in Advertising," and "Charges for Services") that were omitted from this edition because they were outdated. 201 pp.

410. Funke, Otto. *The Piano and How to Care for It: Piano Tuning in Theory and Practice*. Translated by W. London and C. H. Wehlau. Das Musikinstrument Technical Book Series, vol. 6. Frankfurt am Main: Das Musikinstrument, 1961.

Discusses general construction and maintenance of the piano. Although the book includes technical tips on tuning, it is primarily intended to prepare piano owners to communicate with piano technicians. 70 pp.

411. Furey, J. *The Building of the Piano*. London: Musical Opinion, 1929.

> Published by the proprietors of *Musical Opinion*. Discusses the construction process of the piano, from drafting the scale to the final regulation and finishing. Addresses uprights, grands, and "export" pianos (pianos intended for use in extreme climates). Photographs, illustrations (many labeled). 78 pp.

Galpin, Francis W. *A Textbook of European Musical Instruments: Their Origin, History, and Character. See 68 under* History—General History.

Golightly, John Wesley. "The Piano between 1800 and 1850: The Instruments for Which the Composers Wrote." *See 75 under* History—General History.

Good, Edwin M. *Giraffes, Black Dragons, and Other Pianos: A Technological History from Cristofori to the Modern Concert Grand. See 76 under* History—General History.

"A Grand Piano Is Born—A Story of Art and Industry." *See 80 under* History—General History.

412. Haines, Aubrey B. "The Story behind the Piano." *Music Journal* 15, no. 7 (September 1957): 34, 70–71.

> An introductory article about the construction of the piano with a focus on the materials used. Includes some comments about the basic maintenance of the piano.

Halfpenny, Eric. "The Later History of the 'Square.'" *See 84 under* History—General History.

413. Hasluck, Paul N[ooncree]. *Pianos: Their Construction, Tuning, and Repair, with Numerous Engravings and Diagrams*. London: Cassell, 1911.

Topics include construction, purchase and selection, maintenance and repair (tuning, action repairs, restringing, polishing and refinishing, and polishing and recovering keys), and tools. Illustrations (some labeled). 160 pp.

414. Hoskins, Leslie J. "Do All Pianos Sound Alike? Some Background Information to Review before Shopping for That New Piano." *Clavier* 5, no. 5 (October 1966): 52–53.

An overview of some factors that affect the sound of a piano.

415. Hurren, S. A. "From Finger-Tip to Soundboard." *Music Teacher and Piano Student* 39, no. 10 (October 1960): 508.

Discusses the general construction of the piano, with a focus on the sounding mechanisms and the action. Also discusses pedals.

416. ———. "The Instrument We Use." *Music Teacher and Piano Student* 33, no. 9 (September 1954): 403. Reprint, *Music Teacher and Piano Student* 38, no. 8 (August 1959): 357, 371.

An essay about the construction of the piano. Discusses the scale, the frame, the soundboard, strings, pedals, and the action.

417. Kuerti, Anton. "What Pianists Should Know about Pianos." *Clavier* 12, no. 5 (May–June 1973): 12–19.

An overview of the mechanics of the piano, primarily for performers who need to communicate with technicians. Discusses action, extraneous noises, voicing, and strings. Includes a detailed and labeled illustration of the grand piano action, with glossary of terms used for action parts.

Krehbiel, Henry Edward. *The Pianoforte and Its Music. See 101 under* History—General History.

418. Lawrence, Harold. "The Piano vs. the Harpsichord." *Audio* 43, no. 2 (February 1959): 70–71.

An introductory article describing the differences between the harpsichord and the piano.

419. Mason, Merle [H.], comp. *Piano Parts and Their Functions (Illustrated)*. [2nd ed.] Seattle: Piano Technicians Guild, 1981.

Illustrations by James E. Campbell. Originally published in 1977. Labeled diagrams of pianos and piano parts, and glossaries of terms related to piano construction and technology. Includes both vertical and grand pianos. 98 pp.

420. McCombie, Ian. *The Piano Handbook*. 1st American ed. New York: Charles Scribner's Sons, 1980.

Discusses the construction, maintenance, and repair of the piano (uprights, grands, and early pianos). Part 1 is dedicated to the construction of the piano, discussing purchase and selection, piano tone, and the action. Part 2 covers tuning, repair, and cleaning, as well as reconditioning player pianos. Appendix 1 lists piano manufacturers absorbed by other companies, and graded selective list of piano brands. Appendix 2 gives measurements of piano wires, tuning pins, bridge pins, center pins, and key pins. Appendix 3 is a metric conversion table. Photographs, illustrations (many labeled). Glossary, bibliography. 176 pp.

421. McMorrow, Edward. *The Educated Piano: The Structural Relationships and Specifications Essential for Fine Piano Tone*. Edmonds, Wash.: Light Hammer Press, 1989.

Covers construction and maintenance. Discusses materials and mechanics, tuning and temperament, voicing, regulation, and other service procedures. Focuses on the Light Hammer Tone Regulation (LHTR) technique. Addresses both grands and verticals. Topics include tools and materials, troubleshooting, and other professional tips. Photographs, illustrations. Glossary, bibliography. 160 pp.

422. Miller, Harold. *The Rise and Decline of the Piano: Care and Use of the Piano*. Toronto: by the author, n.d.

Explains the general construction of the piano. Discusses the actions of upright and grand pianos, history of tuning and temperament, basic maintenance and care, purchasing, touch and tone. Photographs (labeled). Bibliography. 105 pp.

423. "Music Trade Forum: Grand or Upright?" *Musical Opinion and Music Trade Review* 82, no. 977 (February 1959): 357.

Compares problems of smaller grand pianos to those of the larger grands. Discusses advantages of grands over upright pianos.

424. "Music Trade Forum: The Iron Frame and the Strings." *Musical Opinion* 89, no. 1064 (May 1966): 513.

Explains the basic construction of the piano and some causes of damage to strings and the iron frame.

425. "Music Trade Forum: The Piano of the Future." *Musical Opinion* 86, no. 1025 (February 1963): 317.

An essay discussing the current (as of the publication) challenges in piano construction and speculating on the future developments of the piano.

426. "Music Trade Forum: Tone Appreciation." *Musical Opinion* 89, no. 1061 (February 1966): 321.

Discusses constructional differences between the early piano and the modern piano that contribute to the difference in tone.

427. Nalder, Lawrence M[arcus]. *The Modern Piano.* [London: Musical Opinion], 1927. Reprint, with an introduction by Robert Morgan. London: Heckscher & Co., 1989.

Covers the construction of the modern piano. Addresses both grands and uprights. Discusses pedals, frame, action, hammers, keyboard, and soundboard. Also discusses piano tone and touch, pitch standards, and experimental or unusual pianos (the Janko keyboard, the Emanuel Moór piano, and quarter-tone pianos). Photographs, illustrations (many labeled). 192 pp.

428. Nash, N. "Only the Cream of Forest Products Must Be Used in the Construction of All Types of Pianos." *Piano and Organ Review*

116, no. 7 (July 1957): 20–22; no. 9 (September 1957): 24–26; no. 12 (December 1957): 32–33.

Reprinted from an article titled "Music Grows on Trees" in *The National Hardwood Magazine*. An introduction to the construction of the piano with a focus on wood parts. Addresses wood processing and functions of the parts. Particular attention is paid to the case, soundboard, action, keys, bridge, and wrest plank. The article concludes by promoting piano education, partly because dissemination of pianos benefits the lumber industry.

429. Norton, Edward Quincy. *The Construction, Tuning and Care of the Piano-Forte*. Philadelphia: Oliver Ditson, 1915.

Topics include construction, problem diagnostics and repairs, tuning and temperament, action (English and French) regulation, voicing, basic care, and tools for maintenance and repair. Addresses grands and uprights. A chapter on cabinet organs is included at the end. A labeled illustration of actions. 117 pp.

430. Piano Technicians' Conference. *Secrets of Piano Construction*. Vestal, N.Y.: Vestal Press, 1985.

A reprint of *Proceedings of the Piano Technicians' Conference*, originally published by the American Steel and Wire Company in 1916, 1917, 1918, and 1919, under the title *Piano Tone Building*. Discusses piano construction, materials (woods, felts, wires), varnish, and other tuner-technicians' issues. Includes member lists of Piano Technicians' Conference. Photographs, illustrations (some labeled). 292 pp.

*Piano Technicians Journal. See 24 under* General.

431. "Points about the Piano." *Music Teacher and Piano Student* 31, no. 12 (December 1952): 575.

Discusses construction, maintenance, and repair of the piano. Topics include tuning and the tuner's task, minor repairs, regulation, and adjustment.

Pollens, Stewart. "Early Nineteenth-Century German-Language Works on Piano Maintenance: A Review of Published Information Concerning the Stringing, Tuning, and Adjustment of the Fortepiano." *See 172 under* History—Austria and Germany.

―――. *The Early Pianoforte. See 124 under* History—General History.

Ratcliffe, Ronald V. "Early Pianos: Performance Problems on Pre-1850 Instruments." *See 125 under* History—General History.

―――. "Milestones or Millstones? Upright Pianos of the Past." *See 127 under* History—General History.

432. Rawlings, Kim. *The Best Piano Buyer's Guide.* Salt Lake City, Utah: Sunset Publishing, 1997.

Topics include considerations for selecting a piano for purchase (such as the intended user, space, used versus new, vertical versus grand, the condition of the piano and its parts, warranties, and service), construction of the piano (both vertical and grand), and basic care and maintenance (such as climate control, cleaning, and tuning). A summary list of selection tips. A table of specifications for selected piano brands. Illustrations (labeled). 57 pp.

433. Reblitz, Arthur A. *Piano Servicing, Tuning, and Rebuilding: For the Professional, the Student, and the Hobbyist.* With a preface by Harvey N. Roehl. 2nd ed. Vestal, N.Y.: Vestal Press, 1993.

Topics include history and construction, evaluating old pianos, minor repair and maintenance, regulation, tuning theory and procedure, and restoration. The appendix includes a drill size chart and a conversion table (inches to millimeters). Photographs, illustrations (many labeled). Bibliography. 327 pp.

434. Reed, Jean Ellis. "Construction Features of the Modern Piano." M.M. thesis, Eastman School of Music of the University of Rochester, 1960.

Topics include acoustics, strings and scale design, the soundboard, case, the principles and mechanics of the action, and the history of the instrument. The appendix is an index of piano makers and their patents (if any). Illustrations (many labeled). Bibliography. 51 pp.

Ritzenhein, Mark Steven. "Fortepiano Design and Construction." *See 173 under* History—Austria and Germany.

435. Rosencrantz, I[sidor] B[ertram]. *The Piano: Its Construction, and Relation to Tone, Pitch and Temperament, with Directions How to Use the "Tunella" in Conjunction with the Piano, to Learn the Art of Piano Tuning.* Chicago: The Tunella Company, 1902.

In two parts. The first part is an overview of piano construction, tuning, and temperament. The second part contains directions for tuning the piano by using the Tunella, an electronic tuning device. Photographs, illustrations. 32 pp.

436. Rostkoski, David. "Taming the Temperamental Tyrant: A Piano Technician Speaks Out." *American Music Teacher* 41, no. 1 (August–September 1991): 28–31, 64–65.

An introduction to the maintenance and basic mechanics of the piano. A labeled illustration of the grand action.

Rowland, David, ed. *The Cambridge Companion to the Piano. See 132 under* History—General History.

437. Sadie, Stanley, ed. *The New Grove Dictionary of Music and Musicians.* 20 vols. London: Macmillan, 1980.

See under names of individual parts. Articles are generally brief and may address topics such as the function and purpose of the part, factors that affect its function, and materials used for the part.

Schimmel, Nikolaus. *Piano Manufacturing—An Art and a Craft. See 137 under* History—General History.

438. Schmeckel, Carl D. *The Piano Owner's Guide: How to Buy and*

*Care for a Piano*. Rev. ed. New York: Charles Scribner's Sons, 1974.

Intended for piano owners or prospective owners. Topics include selection, purchase, and basic maintenance of the piano. Focuses on vertical pianos, although grand pianos are also discussed. In four parts. Part 1 contains general information about pianos, such as cost, size, and basic construction, and answers several frequently asked questions. Part 2 addresses some concerns in purchasing a new piano. Part 3 addresses some concerns in purchasing a used piano. Part 4 discusses basic maintenance and care of the piano, such as cleaning, pest control, the placement of the instrument, and obtaining professional services (tuning, regulating, voicing, and other miscellaneous services). Illustrations (labeled). 127 pp.

439. Shead, Herbert A. *The Anatomy of the Piano*. Paperback ed. With a foreword by J. W. T. Roope. Old Woking, England: Unwin Brothers, 1978.

An illustrated dictionary of piano construction. All parts of the instrument are illustrated, many detailed and labeled. Photographs. Bibliography. 177 pp.

————. "Notes on the Historical Background and the Working of the Modern Piano." *See 141 under* History—General History.

Siepmann, Jeremy. *The Piano. See 143 under* History—General History.

Smith, Fanny Morris. *A Noble Art: Three Lectures on the Evolution and Construction of the Piano. See 144 under* History—General History.

440. Snyder, Steven R. *The Piano Owner's Manual*. Marina del Rey, Calif.: SRS Co., 1982.

Discusses general construction and maintenance. Topics include piano types, cleaning, minor repairs, and tuning. Glossary. Illustrations (many labeled). 76 pp.

Tasciotti, Lou. "The Technician's View." *See 309 and 310 under* Builders and Manufacturers—Fandrich.

Tittle, Martin B. "How Grand Pianos Are Made." *See 381 under* Builders and Manufacturers—Story & Clark.

*Tuners' Journal. See 34 under* General.

441. Turner, Earle M. "The Fundamentals of Piano Servicing." *Musical Merchandise Review* 117, no. 2 (February 1958): 70, 73.

Covers the general construction of the piano. Discusses string lengths, the four major parts (back frame, soundboard, strings, and action), the plate, the assembly process, and basic care and maintenance of the piano.

"What's Inside a Piano?" *See 150 under* History—General History.

442. White, William Braid. *Theory and Practice of Piano Construction: With a Detailed, Practical Method for Tuning.* New York: Dover Publications, 1975.

A reprint of the work originally published under the title *Theory and Practice of Pianoforte Building* (New York: Edward Lyman Bill, 1906). Discusses the history, construction, acoustics, tuning and temperament, and some maintenance of the modern piano. Addresses both grands and uprights. Appendices discuss the player piano and smaller grands (five to six feet long) that were popular at the time of the original publication. Illustrations (many labeled). 160 pp.

443. Willis, Aubrey. *Aubrey Willis Home Study Course in Piano Tuning and Repairing.* Orlando, Fla.: by the author, 1968.

Discusses construction, theory and procedures of tuning, regulation, various repairs, refinishing, tools and supplies, and business tips. Addresses grands, uprights, and spinets. Includes a list of suggested books. 118 pp.

444. Wolfenden, Samuel. *A Treatise on the Art of Pianoforte Con-*

*struction.* Rev. ed. With an introduction by David S. Grover and a preface by Frank W. Holland. Old Woking, England: Unwin Brothers, 1977.

Originally published in 1916; revised from the 1975 reprint that also included the supplement published in 1927. Discusses scales, parts of the piano, tuning, voicing, and other topics in construction and maintenance of a piano. The appendix contains some additional notes. The supplement includes additional chapters on tuning, tone, strings, glue, wood screws, and the soundboard. Photographs, illustrations, tables. 274 pp.

445. Woollard, Horace. *The Making of a Modern Pianoforte.* London: John Bale, Sons & Danielsson, [1949].

Explains the construction process of the piano, from the materials used to the final voicing and regulation. Discusses verticals and grands. Illustrations. 51 pp.

# Acoustics

446. Askenfelt, Anders, ed. *Five Lectures on the Acoustics of the Piano.* Publications Issued by the Royal Swedish Academy of Music, no. 64. Stockholm: Royal Swedish Academy of Music, 1990.

A collection of articles about piano construction and acoustics. Addresses general construction, actions and hammers, strings, soundboards, and effects of voicing. Analyses of piano sounds. Photographs, illustrations, graphs. Bibliography at the end of each article. Includes a CD of sound examples. 105 pp.

447. Blackham, E. Donnell. "The Physics of the Piano." *Scientific American* 213, no. 6 (December 1965): 88–99.

Explains the acoustical properties of the piano, with emphasis on inharmonicity. Includes a brief discussion about the history and the construction of the instrument. Illustrations, graphs.

Brinsmead, Edgar. *The History of the Pianoforte: With an Account of*

*the Theory of Sound and Also of the Music and Musical Instru-*
*ments of the Ancients. See 45 under* History—General History.

448. Campbell, Murray, and Clive Greated. *The Musician's Guide to*
*Acoustics.* 1st American ed. New York: Schirmer Books, 1988.

First published by J. M. Dent & Sons in 1987. Includes a
chapter on string keyboard instruments with a section about the
piano (both grands and uprights), which discusses construction,
history, spectrum structure, and tuning. Photographs, illustrations.
A general bibliography and an annotated bibliography on musical
acoustics. 613 pp.

449. Fine, Larry. "The Piano Technician: Acoustical Ingredients of
Tonal Color." *Keyboard* 13, no. 9 (September 1987): 135, 154.

An introductory article about the acoustics of the piano,
particularly about inharmonicity. Illustration.

450. ———. "The Piano Technician: Attack and Decay: Fingerprints
of Piano Tone." *Keyboard* 13, no. 11 (November 1987): 130, 151.

Discusses the acoustics of the piano and the characteristics of
the piano sound.

451. Hall, Donald E. "Piano String Excitation II: General Solution for a
Hard Narrow Hammer." *Journal of the Acoustical Society of*
*America* 81, no. 2 (February 1987): 535–46.

An analytical paper discussing the general solution for a hard
point hammer with a finite mass hitting a perfectly flexible string.
Intended for readers with in-depth knowledge of acoustics.
Illustrations.

452. ———. "Piano String Excitation III: General Solution for a Soft
Narrow Hammer." *Journal of the Acoustical Society of America*
81, no. 2 (February 1987): 547–55.

An analytical paper discussing the general solution for a soft
point hammer with a finite mass hitting a perfectly flexible string.

Intended for readers with in-depth knowledge of acoustics.
Illustrations.

453. ———. "Piano String Excitation in the Case of Small Hammer
Mass." *Journal of the Acoustical Society of America* 79, no. 1
(January 1986): 141–47.

An analytical paper on piano string motion given a very light
hammer (thus short contact time with the string). Intended for
readers with in-depth knowledge of acoustics. Illustrations.

454. Hall, Donald E., and Anders Askenfelt. "Piano String Excitation
V: Spectra for Real Hammers and Strings." *Journal of the
Acoustical Society of America* 83, no. 4 (April 1988): 1627–38.

A technical paper reporting an experimental study on hammer
properties, hammer accelerations, and string motion on a grand
piano. Intended for readers with in-depth knowledge of acoustics.
Illustrations.

455. Hall, Donald E., and Peter Clark. "Piano String Excitation IV: The
Question of Missing Modes." *Journal of the Acoustical Society of
America* 82, no. 6 (December 1987): 1913–18.

A technical paper reporting an experimental study on the
"missing modes" supposedly caused by hammers striking the
piano strings at certain fractions of their lengths. Intended for
readers with in-depth knowledge of acoustics. Illustrations.

456. Hansing, Siegfried. *The Pianoforte and Its Acoustic Properties.*
Rev. and enl. 2nd ed. Translated by Emmy Hansing-Perzina.
Schwerin, Germany: by the author, 1904.

Originally published in German in 1888. Discusses piano parts
and their roles in the acoustical properties of the piano. Also
includes a chapter on basic acoustics and properties of musical
sound, as well as a chapter on repairing pianos (squares, uprights,
and grands). Illustrations. 223 pp.

457. Helmholtz, Hermann L. F. *On the Sensations of Tone as a
Physiological Basis for the Theory of Music.* 2nd rev. English ed.

Translated and revised by Alexander J. Ellis. With an introduction by Henry Margenau. New York: Dover Publications, 1954.

Original English edition published in 1885 (the fourth, and last, German edition published in 1877). Discusses the general acoustical properties of sound and the relationship to tonal harmony. Includes a short section about piano construction and acoustics. Illustrations, tables. 576 pp.

458. Kent, Earle L., ed. *Musical Acoustics: Piano and Wind Instruments*. Benchmark Papers in Acoustics, vol. 9. Stroudsburg, Pa.: Dowden, Hutchinson, and Ross, 1977.

A collection of articles about the construction of musical instruments and the influence on the acoustics of the instruments. The articles are reprinted from various journals (mostly acoustical journals). Part 1 of this three-part work is dedicated to the piano. The topics range from the construction of the piano to the mathematics of vibration. Photographs, illustrations, tables and graphs. Bibliography. 367 pp.

459. McFerrin, W. V. *The Piano—Its Acoustics*. Boston: Tuners Supply Co., 1972.

Topics include history, strings and their properties, harmonics, partials and overtones, timbre, beats, dissonance and resonance, scale and downbearing of a piano, humidity and its effect on the acoustics of the instrument, room acoustics, tuning fork, and hearing. Illustrations (some labeled). The appendix includes a bibliography, a glossary, action diagrams, and tables. 193 pp.

460. "Music Trade Forum: More about Good Tone." *Musical Opinion and Music Trade Review* 83, no. 987 (December 1959): 221.

Explains the acoustical behavior of the piano strings, particularly relative to the strike points.

461. "Music Trade Forum: Resonance in the Piano." *Musical Opinion and Music Trade Review* 77, no. 922 (July 1954): 621.

An introductory article about the acoustics of the piano with a focus on the soundboard.

462. "Music Trade Forum: Smooth Tone and Rough Tone." *Musical Opinion and Music Trade Review* 83, no. 989 (February 1960): 373.

An introductory article about the physics of sound, particularly, the piano sound.

463. "Music Trade Forum: Tone and the Soundboard." *Musical Opinion* 87, no. 1043 (August 1964): 693.

Discusses the construction of the piano with respect to the acoustics, with a focus on the soundboard.

464. Neupert, W. D. "Investigation of the Structure-Borne Sound of Pianos in Homes." *Musik international—Instrumentenbau-Zeitschrift* 38, no. 6 (June 1984): 461–62.

Addresses the problem of piano sound transmitted through conduction (rather than air) and issues in soundproofing.

465. Podlesak, Michael, and Anthony R. Lee. "Dispersion of Waves in Piano Strings." *Journal of the Acoustical Society of America* 83, no. 1 (January 1988): 305–17.

A technical paper reporting an experimental study about wave dispersion. Intended for readers with in-depth knowledge of acoustics. Photograph, illustrations.

466. Rasch, Rudolf A., and Vincent Heetvelt. "String Inharmonicity and Piano Tuning." *Music Perception* 3, no. 2 (Winter 1985): 171–89.

An article about inharmonicity of piano strings and its effect on tuning. Extensive discussion of the mathematical basis of inharmonicity. Graphs. Bibliography.

467. Rossing, Thomas D., ed. *Musical Acoustics: Selected Reprints.*

College Park, Md.: American Association of Physics Teachers, 1988.

Contains reprints of articles from various journals. The two articles specifically about the piano are "Coupled Piano Strings" by Gabriel Weinreich, pp. 73–83; and "Acoustical Research on Pianos: I. Vibrational Characteristics of the Soundboard" by Klaus Wogram, translated by Jakob Engelhardt, pp. 85–98 (bibliography at the end of the article). Both are classified under string instruments. Graphs. 227 pp.

Rowland, David, ed. *The Cambridge Companion to the Piano. See 132 under* History—General History.

468. Sadie, Stanley, ed. *The New Grove Dictionary of Music and Musicians*. London: Macmillan, 1980. S.v. "Acoustics," by Ronald Lewcock, John C. Schelleng, Carleen M. Hutchins, Daniel W. Martin, Arthur Benade, and Johan Sundberg.

Includes a short section on the piano under "keyboards." Illustrations. Bibliography.

469. Young, Robert W. "Inharmonicity of Plain Wire Piano Strings." *Journal of the Acoustical Society of America* 24, no. 3 (May 1952): 267–73.

An experimental study on inharmonicity. Discusses the theory of inharmonicity and properties of piano string inharmonicity. Measurements were taken on Steinway as well as other pianos. Intended for readers with in-depth knowledge of acoustics. Illustrations.

# Action

Bargreen, Melinda. "Taking Action: Seattleites' Revolutionary Invention Is Music to the Ears of Pianists." *See 306 under* Builders and Manufacturers—Fandrich.

Cotter, Marianne. "New Respect for the Upright Piano." *See 308 under*

Builders and Manufacturers—Fandrich.

470. Davis, F. Kelso. "The Modern Piano Action." *Music Journal* 23, no. 2 (February 1965): 52, 93.

An introductory essay about the modern piano action. Photographs.

471. Dietz, Franz Rudolf. *Das Regulieren von Flügeln bei Steinway* (The Regulation of the Steinway Grand Action). 3rd ed. Frankfurt am Main: Das Musikinstrument, 1981.

English translation by Peter Reisiger and J. M. Hill. Discusses the construction of the action and steps in regulating the Steinway action. In German, English, French, Italian, and Swedish. English text on pp. 25–39. Thirty-eight photographs. 82 pp.

472. Esterowitz, M[ichael]. "Piano Doctor: Bad Action." *Keyboard Classics* 4, no. 2 (March–April 1984): 41.

Explains the basic mechanics of the action and regulation. Also discusses differences between grands and uprights.

473. ———. "Piano Doctor: Ready for Action!" *Keyboard Classics* 3, no. 6 (November–December 1983): 39.

Discusses the mechanics of the vertical piano action. Illustration (labeled).

474. ———. "Piano Doctor: The Grand Action." *Keyboard Classics* 4, no. 1 (January–February 1984): 41.

Explains the construction and mechanics of the grand piano action. Illustration (labeled).

475. Fine, Larry. "The Piano Technician: Action Design, Materials, & Manufacturing." *Keyboard* 11, no. 9 (September 1985): 77.

Discusses differences in upright and grand actions, quality of actions, materials used, and tips for evaluating actions when purchasing a piano. Illustration.

476. ———. "The Piano Technician: Where the Action Is—The Invisible Differences between Vertical Piano Types." *Keyboard* 11, no. 7 (July 1985): 79.

Discusses the differences in the action among vertical piano types with special attention to the disadvantages of the spinet action. Illustration.

477. Johannesen, Grant. "Ups and Downs of Piano Action." *Music Journal* 26, no. 2 (February 1968): 26, 66.

Includes a discussion addressing considerations about the action in selecting a piano.

"Knuckle Under!" *See 345 under* Builders and Manufacturers—Seiler.

Latcham, Michael. "The Check in Some Early Pianos and the Development of Piano Technique around the Turn of the 18th Century." *See 102 under* History—General History.

478. Levine, Henry. "The Key to Piano Playing." *Clavier* 6, no. 5 (May–June 1967): 12–16, 19–20.

Discusses piano playing from the mechanical view of the instrument. An overview of the grand piano action. Illustrations. See "The Grand Piano Action" by Thomas Porter (pp. 17–19) for additional illustrations.

479. "Music Trade Forum: Action Parts." *Musical Opinion and Music Trade Review* 76, no. 903 (December 1952): 189.

An essay about the merits of manufacturing piano actions by machinery and specialization.

480. "Music Trade Forum: Grand Action Methods." *Musical Opinion* 88, no. 1053 (June 1965): 577; no. 1054 (July 1965): 641.

Discusses single escapement and double escapement actions and issues in regulating them.

481. Pfeiffer, Walter. *The Piano Key and Whippen: An Analysis of*

*Their Relationships in Direct Blow Actions.* With a preface and translated by Jim Engelhardt. Fachbuchreihe Das Musikinstrument (Das Musikinstrument Technical Book Series), vol. 18. Frankfurt am Main: Das Musikinstrument, 1967.

Detailed scientific discussions. Topics include contacting profiles, forces, balance point, key dip, and travel. Illustrations. 73 pp.

482. Porter, Thomas. "The Grand Piano Action." *Clavier* 6, no. 5 (May–June 1967): 17–19.

Supplements "The Key to Piano Playing," by Henry Levine (pp. 12–16, 19–20). Explains how the grand action works.

Ratcliffe, Ronald V. "Where the Action Is: How It Affects the Performer." *See 128 under* History—General History.

Savard, David M. "88+34 Years above the Piano Stool: The Steinway Grand Action, 1979." *See 372 under* Builders and Manufacturers—Steinway.

"Seiler Applies New Technologies to Grand Piano Construction." *See 346 under* Builders and Manufacturers—Seiler.

"Seiler Uprights: Patented New Action Offers Faster Speed of Repetition." *See 347 under* Builders and Manufacturers—Seiler.

483. Shead, Herbert [A.]. "How the Piano Works." *Music Teacher and Piano Student* 31, no. 2 (February 1952): 76–77.

Explains the basic construction and design of the piano action. Illustrations (labeled).

Strauch Brothers. *The Manufacture of Pianoforte Action: Its Rise and Development. See 146 under* History—General History.

## Case and Frame

"Currier's Radical New SSP 'Plate-Less' Piano." *See 292 under* Builders and Manufacturers—Currier.

484. Distler, Jed. "The Instrument: Art-Case Piano Designs." *Piano & Keyboard* no. 192 (May–June 1998): 62–63.

An article on John Diebboll and his unique piano case designs. Illustrations.

485. Fine, Larry. "The Piano Technician: Quality & Sophistication in Piano Cabinetry." *Keyboard* 11, no. 5 (May 1985): 64.

Discusses cabinetry design (including materials used) and its relationship to the quality of the piano.

486. "Industry Briefings: Two-Lidded Grand Piano Causes Uproar." *Music Trades* 146, no. 2 (March 1998): 22.

A brief report on the lower lid for grand pianos invented by Daniell Revenaugh.

487. Montandon, Blaise. "Keyboard Topography." *Clavier* 1, no. 5 (November–December 1962): 17–18.

Addresses the physical appearance and the outer design of the piano. Discusses applications for performance and teaching.

Møller, Dorthe Falcon. "C. C. Hornung and the Single-Cast Iron Frame: An Early Break-Through in the Danish Piano Industry." *See 319 under* Builders and Manufacturers—Hornung, Conrad Christian

488. "Music Trade Forum: Continental Finish." *Musical Opinion and Music Trade Review* 83, no. 990 (March 1960): 445.

Instructions for the German and Viennese method of varnishing and its variants (including the "American" method).

489. "Music Trade Forum: French Polishing." *Musical Opinion and Music Trade Review* 79, no. 937 (October 1955): 61; no. 938

(November 1955): 125.

Instructions on touching up slight scratches with French polish. Also addresses some issues associated with finishing.

490. "Music Trade Forum: The Convenience of French Polishing." *Musical Opinion* 84, no. 1003 (April 1961): 461.

Explains the procedures of French polishing and its advantages over other methods.

491. "Music Trade Forum: The Decline of French Polishing." *Musical Opinion and Music Trade Review* 78, no. 936 (September 1955): 766.

Discusses advantages and disadvantages of French polishing.

492. "Music Trade Forum: The Piano Frame." *Musical Opinion* 84, no. 1005 (June 1961): 589.

Addresses issues concerning the cast-iron frames and their effects on the piano.

493. "Music Trade Forum: The Three Methods of Polishing." *Musical Opinion* 87, no. 1036 (January 1964): 253.

An introductory article about finishing, comparing different methods (French polishing, varnishing, and using synthetic polish).

494. "To Make It Perfectly Clear." *Music [&] Artists* 4, no. 5 (December 1971–January 1972): 2.

A brief report on the glass lid designed to fit both Steinway and Baldwin grands, intended for concerto performances.

# Dampers

495. Dotzek, D. H. "Damper Assembly with D. F. A. System." *Musik international—Instrumentenbau-Zeitschrift* 37, no. 8 (August 1983): 523–24.

Explains a method of fitting the dampers devised by the author. Illustration (labeled).

496. "Music Trade Forum: Dampers." *Musical Opinion* 85, no. 1020 (September 1962): 765.

Discusses difference in damper mechanisms between grands and uprights and repair procedures for each. [Note: This article is not a reprint of the article by the same title in vol. 79, no. 945 (June 1956).]

## Hammers

497. Dreier, Thomas. *Sheep's Wool and Paderewski*. Boston: American Felt Company, 1917.

Discusses hammer felt processing and piano hammer making. Includes a brief history of hammer felt making in the United States. Photographs. 46 pp.

498. Fine, Larry. "The Piano Technician: Piano Hammers: Another Favorite Site for Sales Gimmicks." *Keyboard* 11, no. 11 (November 1985): 85.

Discusses the construction of piano hammers and considerations for purchasing a piano. Illustrations.

499. "Music Trade Forum: Hammer Coverings." *Musical Opinion and Music Trade Review* 82, no. 978 (March 1959): 429.

Addresses felt used in pianos with a focus on hammer felt. Includes a brief history of hammer coverings.

500. "Music Trade Forum: Tone-Preserving." *Musical Opinion* 87, no. 1033 (October 1963): 61.

Explains factors that affect the tone of the piano. Addresses scale design, downbearing pressure, soundboard, strike points on the strings, and hammer felts.

501. Pfeiffer, Walter. *The Piano Hammer: A Detailed Investigation into an Important Facet of Piano Manufacturing with 91 Figures and 4 Graphs*. Translated by J. Engelhardt. With a foreword by Helmut Pfeiffer. Das Musikinstrument Technical Book Series, vol. 34. Frankfurt am Main: Das Musikinstrument, 1978.

Discusses types of hammer action, jack and let-off, hammer weight, volume of sound, and measuring properties of hammer travel. The original German edition was published in 1948. Bibliography. 118 pp.

## Keys

"High Notes." *See 329 under* Builders and Manufacturers—Laurence and Nash.

502. Donison, Christopher. "The Instrument: Small Hands? Try This Keyboard, You'll Like It." *Piano & Keyboard* no. 193 (July–August 1998): 41–43.

Discusses the motivation behind the Donison-Steinbuhler Standard keyboard, a seven-eighth size keyboard that fits any piano.

503. Reimann, Hannah. "Point of View: A Modest Proposal." *Piano Today* 17, no. 4 (Fall 1997): 12–13.

A short history of the key widths. Discusses several custom-made pianos with narrower keys.

"The Talk of the Town: Change of Keys." *See 378 under* Builders and Manufacturers—Steinway.

"World View: Steinway Explores Ivory Substitute." *See 380 under* Builder and Manufacturers—Steinway.

# Pedals

Bilson, Malcolm. "The Soft Pedal Revisited." *See 41 under* History—General History.

Edwards, Miriam. "Pedal for Pianists." *See 58 under* History—General History.

504. Fine, Larry. "The Piano Technician: All about Pedals." *Keyboard* 11, no. 12 (December 1985): 100.

Addresses the differences between grand pedals and vertical pedals. Discusses damper pedals, *una corda* pedals (grands), "soft" pedal (uprights), sostenuto pedals, and practice pedals (uprights), and their presence/absence in relation to the quality of the piano. Also discusses trapwork. Illustrations.

Houck, Margaret A. "The History and Development of the Sostenuto Pedal and Its Use in Selected 20th-Century Repertoire." *See 96 under* History—General History.

505. Hyman, Dick. "The Mysterious Middle Pedal." *Keyboard Classics & Piano Stylist* 15, no. 2 (March–April 1995): 25, 36, 48.

Explains the function and use of the sostenuto pedal. Includes an overview of the history of piano pedals.

506. "Music Trade Forum: The Middle Pedal." *Musical Opinion and Music Trade Review* 78, no. 925 (October 1954): 61.

Discusses the use, the mechanism, maintenance, and the controversies over the sostenuto pedal.

Rowland, David. *A History of Pianoforte Pedalling. See 133 under* History—General History.

507. Tasciotti, Lou. "The Technician's View." *Piano Quarterly* 40, no. 155 (Fall 1991): 52–54.

Detailed explanations of the pedals found on the modern piano. Discusses both vertical and grand pianos.

Wolfram, Victor. *The Sostenuto Pedal. See 155 under* History—General History.

## Soundboard

508. Esterowitz, Michael. "The Piano Doctor: Is Your Soundboard Healthy?" *Keyboard Classics* 4, no. 5 (September–October 1984): 41.

    Discusses the basic characteristics and problems of soundboards. Illustration.

509. Fandrich, Delwin. "Are Soundboards All They're Cracked Up to Be?" *Piano Quarterly* 40, no. 158 (Summer 1992): 63–68.

    Discusses cracks, impedance, and the crown. Photographs.

510. Hamerton, Ann. "Of Sounding Boards." *Making Music* no. 45 (Spring 1961): 10.

    Addresses reasons for inferior soundboards in British pianos. Discusses the selection and treatment of wood.

"Music Trade Forum: Resonance in the Piano." *See 461 under Construction and Design*—Acoustics.

"Music Trade Forum: Tone and the Soundboard." *See 463 under Construction and Design*—Acoustics.

"Music Trade Forum: Tone-Preserving." *See 500 under Construction and Design*—Hammers.

"New Piano Soundboard Unveiled by Wurlitzer at NAMM-West." *See 390 under* Builders and Manufacturers—Wurlitzer.

"New Young Chang Soundboards." *See 397 under* Builders and Manufacturers—Young Chang.

"'Perma Crown Tone Board' of Plywood Adopted by Kimball after 12-

Year Test." *See 323 under* Builders and Manufacturers—Kimball.

"Seiler Applies New Technologies to Grand Piano Construction." *See 346 under* Builders and Manufacturers—Seiler.

"Swedish Piano." *See 255 under* Builders and Manufacturers—Bolin, Georg.

## Strings and Scale Design

"Baldwin Granted Two Patents for Bass String Design." *See 241 under* Builders and Manufacturers—Baldwin.

511. Fine, Larry. "The Piano Technician: Scale Design & Strings." *Keyboard* 14, no. 2 (February 1988): 134.

Discusses the basic principles of scale design including string length, mass, and tension. Illustrations.

512. Goddard, W. Trow. *A Handbook on the Strings of the Pianoforte and Other Keyboard Instruments with Design Formulae.* Stockton-on-Tees, England: by the author, 1985.

A detailed reference book about the acoustics of the piano strings (applicable to other instruments). Addresses both unwound and wound (single wound and double wound) strings. Illustrations, tables. 86 pp.

513. "Music Trade Forum: More about Stringing." *Musical Opinion* 86, no. 1030 (July 1963): 637.

Addresses overstringing and other issues in string scale design with some mathematical discussion.

514. "Music Trade Forum: Pianoforte Essentials." *Musical Opinion and Music Trade Review* 77, no. 923 (August 1954): 677.

An introductory article about piano scale design with mathematical discussion.

515. "Music Trade Forum: Piano Wire." *Musical Opinion* 86, no. 1024 (January 1963): 253.

A brief article about the history of piano wire and current standards. Tables of gauge measurements for wires and tuning pins.

"Music Trade Forum: The Evolution of Stringing." *See 171 under* History—Austria and Germany.

"Music Trade Forum: Tone-Preserving." *See 500 under Construction and Design*—Hammers.

Rasch, Rudolf A., and Vincent Heetvelt. "String Inharmonicity and Piano Tuning." *See 466 under Construction and Design*—Acoustics.

516. Roberts, David. *The Calculating Technician.* Kansas City: Piano Technicians Guild Foundation Press, 1990.

Based on a series of articles, "The Calculating Technician," originally printed in *Piano Technicians Journal* from 1979 to 1981. Introduces and explains mathematical formulae related to scale design. Appendices discuss use of calculators (some specific discussions on programmable calculators). Intended for readers trained in the subject. Tables, illustrations. Bibliography. 120 pp.

517. Schadler, John, Jr. "The Necessary Element of Piano Wire to Assure Piano Strings Which Will Produce Quality Tone." *Piano and Organ Review* 116, no. 10 (October 1957): 26–27.

Discusses the steel wires used in pianos. Addresses topics such as dimensions, necessary properties for piano wires, and rust protection.

"Seiler Applies New Technologies to Grand Piano Construction." *See 346 under* Builders and Manufacturers—Seiler.

518. Thomma, Lothar, and Klaus Fenner. *Duplex Slide Rule TF 65/2: For Figuring All Strings for Pianos, Harpsichords etc.* Schriften-

reihe Das Musikinstrument, edited by H. K. Herzog. Frankfurt am Main: Das Musikinstrument, [1983].

Instructions on using the duplex slide rule for string dimensions (diameter, tension, length, etc.), with examples. Tables. 27 pp.

## Miscellaneous

519. Doerschuk, Robert L. "Earth Watch: Sound Thoughts on Spruce Abuse." *Keyboard* 18, no. 3 (March 1992): 29.

A short essay concerning the availability of sitka spruce, the preferred wood for soundboards.

520. Fine, Larry. "The Piano Technician: It's the Real Thing! (Or Is It?)" *Keyboard* 11, no. 4 (April 1985): 78.

Discusses wood and other substitute materials used for piano construction. Illustration.

Mobbs, Kenneth. "Stops and Other Special Effects on the Early Piano." *See 111 under* History—General History.

521. Welbourne, Todd. "The Diagonal Bar Controversy." *Piano Quarterly* 39, no. 154 (Summer 1991): 57–60.

An essay about the diagonal bar (oblique brace) found in some Steinway grand models. Illustrations.

# Maintenance and Repair

## General Maintenance and Repair

522. Agnes, Sister M. "What's Your Score?" *Etude* 69, no. 7 (July 1951): 57.

     Explains the basic care of the piano in a quiz format.

523. American Society of Piano Technicians. "Know Your Piano." *Music of the West Magazine* 7, no. 12 (August 1952): 6.

     Discusses basic maintenance of the piano, such as tuning, cleaning, climate control, and pest control.

524. Ashton, Irene. "Care of the Piano." *Music Teacher and Piano Student* 29, no. 10 (October 1950): 462.

     Discusses climate, cleaning, tuning, and other basic care issues. An abridged version of this script was broadcast on "Woman's Hour" on April 12, 1950.

525. *Baldwin Piano Service Manual: Grands, Studios, Consoles, Spinets*. Cincinnati: Baldwin Piano & Organ Company, 1967.

     Detailed instructions for services such as regulating the action and the pedal, voicing, and replacing the strings. Includes Baldwin, Hamilton, and Howard grand pianos, and Acrosonic, Hamilton, and Howard vertical pianos. Ordering instructions for replacement parts. Detailed and labeled illustrations. Tables of string scales. 27 pp.

Bezdechi, Adrian. *Pianos & Player Pianos: An Informative Guide for Owners and Prospective Buyers. See 400 under* Construction and Design—General Construction.

526. Booth, George W. *Pianos, Piano Tuners and Their Problems.* London: Janus Publishing Company, 1996.

> A collection of problems in maintenance and repair of the piano. Includes case histories. Discusses repairs, special or unusual pianos, new pianos with problems, humidity-related problems, tuning, and business tips. For each case a description of the instrument (make, serial number, date, and dimensions) is given. Primarily intended for tuner-technicians with formal training and experience. Photographs, tables. Bibliography. 208 pp.

527. Bowen, York. "What Is a Good Piano?" *Music Teacher and Piano Student* 31, no. 4 (April 1952): 196. Reprint, *Music Teacher and Piano Student* 37, no. 9 (September 1958): 396.

> Discusses the characteristics of pianos in good condition with respect to the action and the tone.

528. Bradley, Jack. *How to Tune, Repair and Regulate Pianos: A Practical Guide—Illustrated.* 1st ed. South Charleston, W.Va.: Hill Springs Publications, 1986.

> A textbook. Discusses repair, regulation, tuning, and moving the piano, as well as business tips. Includes a list of supply and tool companies, organizations, and piano manufacturers. Photographs, illustrations. Glossary. 156 pp.

529. "Care of the Piano." *Music Teacher* 51, no. 4 (April 1972): 9–10.

> Discusses basic maintenance and care of the piano. Topics include tuning and servicing, humidity control, moving, and cleaning.

530. Colbert, Warren E. *Piano Tuning for Piano Players.* Linthicum Heights, Md.: Lyn-Lee-Lou Publishing, 1985.

> A self-learning guide for procedures and techniques of tuning

and piano repair, targeted at pianists. Discusses both grand and vertical pianos. Photograph, illustrations. 70 pp.

531. Cranmer, Reginald A. "If It's Not Worth Tuning, Chop It Up!" *Making Music* no. 68 (Autumn 1968): 9–12.

Discusses basic care of the piano such as climate control, pests, and working with a tuner-technician. Illustrations (labeled).

532. Fahrer, G. W., Jr. "Beware of the Neglected Piano!" *Music Journal* 18, no. 6 (September 1960): 48.

Explains the effects of storage and neglect on the piano.

Fine, Larry. *The Piano Book: Buying & Owning a New or Used Piano. See 408 under* Construction and Design—General Construction.

533. ———. "The Piano Technician: Final Preparation of a Piano in the Factory—A Difference You Can Really Notice." *Keyboard* 12, no. 2 (February 1986): 97.

Discusses tuning, regulating, voicing, and cleaning. Also discusses considerations in purchasing a piano.

Fischer, J[erry] Cree. *Piano Tuning: A Simple and Accurate Method for Amateurs. See 409 under* Construction and Design—General Construction.

Funke, Otto. *The Piano and How to Care for It: Piano Tuning in Theory and Practice. See 410 under* Construction and Design—General Construction.

534. Goff, Hardy N. *Goff's Money Saving Piano Guide.* Hammond, La.: by the author, 1975.

Discusses selection and purchase, basic care, and minor repairs of the piano, primarily intended for beginners and non-musicians. Includes comments specific to purchasing a piano for church use. Photographs. 23 pp.

535. Grover, David S. "Instruments: Caring for the Piano." *Music in*

*Education* 42, no. 390 (February 1978): 75–76.

Discusses piano care provided by the owner and service provided by a technician. Also discusses moving and storage. Photographs.

536. Guenther, Robert. "How to Ruin Your Favorite Piano." *Clavier* 21, no. 4 (April 1982): 46–47.

Discusses basic care of the piano such as the placement of the instrument in the home, humidity control, cleaning, and when to call for a professional technician.

Hasluck, Paul N[ooncree]. *Pianos: Their Construction, Tuning, and Repair, with Numerous Engravings and Diagrams. See 413 under* Construction and Design—General Construction.

537. Hobbs, H[enry]. *The Piano in India: How to Keep It in Order: Practical Information on Repairing, Regulating, Tuning, Packing, and Treatment of Pianofortes in Tropical Climates.* 2nd ed. Calcutta, India: Thacker, Spink & Co., 1914.

Topics include the selection of a piano, basic care (especially concerning climate and humidity), general construction, problem diagnostics, minor maintenance and repair, and transporting the piano. Discusses grands, uprights, cottage pianos, and squares, as well as player pianos and reed organs. Addresses issues specific to the tropical climate. Primarily intended for non-technicians. Photographs, illustrations (many labeled). 201 pp., plus 7 pp. of advertisements.

538. Holliday, Kent. "Give Your Old Upright a Facelift." *Clavier* 15, no. 5 (May–June 1976): 8–11.

Instructions on cleaning and performing minor repairs on old uprights. Photographs.

539. Hoskins, Leslie J. "Care for Your Piano." *Clavier* 1, no. 4 (October 1962): 18–22.

Discusses construction and general maintenance of the piano.

Topics include humidity, voicing, and regulation. Photographs, illustrations.

540. ———. "Piano Care, Sense and Nonsense." *Musart* 20, no. 5 (April–May 1968): 14, 36–37.

Discusses basic maintenance and care of the piano, intended for nonprofessionals. Addresses the effects of neglect, placement of the instrument, humidity and climate control, cleaning, and selecting a technician.

541. Howe, Alfred H. *Scientific Piano Tuning and Servicing*. 3rd rev. and enl. ed. New York: by the author, 1947.

Topics include tuning procedures, temperament, regulation, voicing, repairs, and general maintenance (uprights and grands). Includes chapters on the organ, the minipiano, and the piano accordion, as well as business tips for piano technicians. Also includes a chapter of anecdotes about tuners. Illustrations (some labeled). Glossaries, bibliography. 267 pp.

542. Jackson, Jim. *Tuning & Repairing Your Own Piano*. Blue Ridge Summit, Pa.: Tab Books, 1984.

Discusses general information about the piano, tuning, acoustics, tools, troubleshooting and repairing, voicing, regulation, and business tips for piano technicians. Includes tuning exercises and a chapter on vertical piano action. The appendix is a list of piano supply companies with their addresses. Photographs, illustrations (many labeled). Glossary. 216 pp.

543. Johnson, Michael, and Robin Mackworth-Young. *Tune and Repair Your Own Piano: A Practical and Theoretical Guide to the Tuning of All Keyboard Stringed Instruments, and to the Running Repair of the Piano*. London: Clavitune, 1978. Reprint, London: Harcourt Brace Jovanovich, 1979.

A guide to the basic tuning, maintenance, and repair of the piano. Discusses the principles and techniques of tuning, general construction of the piano, removing and replacing the action, repairing and replacing bearings and strings, and some common problems with the piano and appropriate repairs. Photograph, illustrations (some are labeled in detail). 82 pp.

Kuerti, Anton. "What Pianists Should Know about Pianos." *See 417 under* Construction and Design—General Construction.

544. Matthias, Max. *Steinway Service Manual: Guide to the Care of a Steinway.* Translated by Thomas Ball. Frankfurt am Main: Verlag Erwin Bochinsky, 1990.

In German (first half of the book) and English (second half of the book). Discusses regulation, tuning, voicing, finishing, tools, and basic care. Includes a list of Steinway serial numbers, tables of string dimensions for Steinway grands and uprights, and table of frequencies. Primarily intended for piano technicians. Photographs, illustrations (many labeled). 152 pp.

McCombie, Ian. *The Piano Handbook. See 420 under* Construction and Design—General Construction.

McGeary, Thomas. "Johann Lehmann's Fortepiano Tuning and Maintenance Manual (1827)." *See 168 under* History—Austria and Germany.

————. "Karl Lemme's Manual on Fortepiano and Clavichord Maintenance (1802)." *See 169 under* History—Austria and Germany.

McMorrow, Edward. *The Educated Piano: The Structural Relationships and Specifications Essential for Fine Piano Tone. See 421 under* Construction and Design—General Construction.

545. Meehan, Joseph A. "Piano Care: Answers to Ten Crucial Questions." *Contemporary Keyboard* 3, no. 6 (June 1977): 10, 34–36.

Explains the basic maintenance and care of the piano in a question-and-answer format. Addresses tuning, placement, cleaning, moving, soundboard cracks, selection of piano tuners, and other miscellaneous topics.

Miller, Harold. *The Rise and Decline of the Piano: Care and Use of the*

*Piano. See 422 under* Construction and Design—General Construction.

546. "Music Trade Forum: Easy Upkeep of the Piano." *Musical Opinion* 84, no. 999 (December 1960): 205.

Explains basic maintenance and care of the piano, primarily intended for nonprofessional readers. Discusses cleaning and checking for broken or worn-out parts.

547. "Music Trade Forum: Piano Care and Maintenance." *Musical Opinion and Music Trade Review* 80, no. 958 (July 1957): 637.

Discusses swollen wooden parts and damp keys due to humidity, unevenness of the keys, and general distortion of the keyboard.

548. "Music Trade Forum: The Minipiano." *Musical Opinion and Music Trade Review* 76, no. 907 (April 1953): 445.

Instructions for servicing a minipiano.

549. "Music Trade Forum: The Modern Piano: Its Care and Maintenance." *Musical Opinion and Music Trade Review* 80, no. 954 (March 1957): 381; no. 955 (April 1957): 445.

Discusses climate control, cleaning the exterior of the piano, and replacing hinges and damaged wood around the hinges.

550. "Music Trade Forum: Unwanted Noises." *Musical Opinion and Music Trade Review* 80, no. 959 (August 1957): 701.

Discusses sympathetic vibrations (both interior and exterior of the piano) and noises from loose hammer heads or shanks.

551. "Music Trade Forum: Unwanted Noises." *Musical Opinion and Music Trade Review* 82, no. 980 (May 1959): 573.

Addresses extraneous noises in the piano such as sympathetic vibrations, noises caused by foreign objects in the piano, and noises in the action. [Note: This article is not a reprint of the article by the same title in vol. 80, no. 959 (August 1957).]

Norton, Edward Quincy. *The Construction, Tuning and Care of the Piano-Forte. See 429 under* Construction and Design—General Construction.

*Piano Technicians Journal. See 24 under* General.

"Points about the Piano." *See 431 under* Construction and Design—General Construction.

552. Porter, Thomas. "A Pianist's Guide to Effective Piano Maintenance." *Clavier* 5, no. 3 (May–June 1966): 19–23.

An overview of piano maintenance, primarily to help performers communicate with technicians. Addresses tuning, cleaning, regulating, voicing, long-term maintenance, and rebuilding. Discusses both uprights and grands. Illustrations.

553. "The Problem with Bad Pianos." *Music Teacher* 62, no. 9 (September 1983): 16.

Addresses some misconceptions about purchase and care of the piano, compiled by the Piano Advisory Board of United Kingdom.

Rawlings, Kim. *The Best Piano Buyer's Guide. See 432 under* Construction and Design—General Construction.

Reblitz, Arthur A. *Piano Servicing, Tuning, and Rebuilding: For the Professional, the Student, and the Hobbyist. See 433 under* Construction and Design—General Construction.

Rostkoski, David. "Taming the Temperamental Tyrant: A Piano Technician Speaks Out." *See 436 under* Construction and Design—General Construction.

554. Salt, J. Peter. "Have You Had Your Piano Tuned Lately?" *Music Teacher* 54, no. 9 (September 1975): 21–22; no. 10 (October 1975): 13–14; no. 11 (November 1975): 18–20.

Topics include tuning and temperament, selecting a piano, and basic maintenance. Although the article includes some technical discussion about tuning, it is primarily intended to help piano owners communicate with technicians.

Schmeckel, Carl D. *The Piano Owner's Guide: How to Buy and Care for a Piano. See 438 under* Construction and Design—General Construction.

555. Scott, Harral. "Give Your Piano a Better Care." *Music Educators Journal* 38, no. 3 (January 1952): 53–54.

A short article about basic piano care.

556. Smith, Eric. *Piano Care and Restoration*. Blue Ridge Summit, Pa.: Tab Books, 1981.

Originally published under the title *Pianos: Care and Restoration* (London: Lutterworth Press, 1980). Discusses repairs and restoration of older pianos. Topics include tools and materials, tone and touch, structure, the action (upright and grand), tuning and voicing, and purchasing and restoring old pianos. Photographs, illustrations (many labeled). Glossary, bibliography. 192 pp.

557. Smith, Virgil E. *Your Piano & Your Piano Technician*. San Diego: Neil A. Kjos, Jr., 1981.

A guide to the maintenance and care of the piano to help piano owners communicate with the piano technician. Discusses reasons for maintenance, selecting a piano, selecting and working with a technician, tuning, the piano action, the hammers, major repairs, reconditioning, and rebuilding. Illustrations. 56 pp.

Snyder, Steven R. *The Piano Owner's Manual. See 440 under* Construction and Design—General Construction.

558. Spillane, Daniel. *The Piano: Scientific, Technical, and Practical Instructions Relating to Tuning, Regulating, and Toning*. New York: Edward Lyman Bill, 1903.

Topics include tuning and temperament, basic acoustics of the piano, voicing and factors that affect the tone, and regulating the action. Discusses uprights, squares, and grands. Illustrations (labeled). 112 pp.

559. Stamm, Gustav W. *Piano Tuning Made Easy: A Practical Step-by-Step Guide*. Kalamazoo, Mich.: Stamm Industries, 1975.

In addition to the step-by-step instructions on tuning, the book discusses construction, pitch and temperament, basic repairs, action regulation, voicing, some acoustical issues, and purchase and selection of a piano. Primarily intended for beginning technicians. Illustrations. 24 pp.

560. Steinway, John H. "Caring for Your Piano." *Virtuoso & Keyboard Classics Magazine* 2, [no. 2] (March–April 1981): 39.

Discusses tuning, climate control, cleaning, and other maintenance topics.

561. Stevens, Floyd A. *Complete Course in Professional Piano Tuning, Repair, and Rebuilding*. Professional/Technical Series. Chicago: Nelson-Hall Publishers, 1972.

Discusses construction and maintenance. Topics include tools and supplies, regulation, tuning and temperament, various repairs, restringing, voicing, and refinishing, business tips, and troubleshooting. Also discusses tuning using an electronic device (Strobotuner). Addresses grands, uprights, and electronic organs and pianos. Photographs, illustrations (many labeled). 216 pp.

562. Tasciotti, Lou. "The Technician's View: Breaking In Versus Breaking Down." *Piano Quarterly* 37, no. 147 (Fall 1989): 47–50.

Discusses deterioration in pianos due to wear and its causes. Topics include hammer wear, wear in the action, and deterioration of the soundboard.

563. Templeton, P. B. *The Handmaid to the Pianoforte: Comprising a Full Description of the Mechanism of the Instrument, the Various Defects to Which It Is Liable, Directions How to Remedy Each*

*Defect, and Instructions How to Keep the Instrument Always in Tune.* Philadelphia: Lee & Walker; Pittsburgh: Henry Kleber & John H. Mellor; New York: Firth, Pond & Co.; Boston: Oliver Ditson, 1851.

Discusses the moving parts of the piano. Topics include evaluating the action, problem diagnostics and repair, and tuning. Includes information specific to some brands (Chickering and Nunns & Clark). 36 pp.

564. Tittle, Martin [B.]. "The Kenzoid—Why Bother?" *Piano Quarterly* 26, no. 100 (Winter 1977–1978): 36–39. Reprint, *Piano Technicians Journal* 21, no. 12 (December 1978): 9–11.

Discusses the four areas of piano service (basic maintenance, tuning, action regulation, and voicing) and their interrelationship, based on the scheme devised by Kenzo Utsunomiya.

565. Travis, John W. *Let's Tune Up: A Study Course for Students of Piano Technology.* 1st ed. With a foreword by Paul Hume. Edited by R. Annabel Rathman. Tacoma Park, Md.: by the author, 1968.

Discusses history, design and construction, temperament, theory and practice of piano tuning, repairs, regulations, and voicing. Includes tips on record keeping. Photographs, illustrations. Glossary, bibliography. 375 pp.

566. Trevor, June. "Church Pianos." *Choir* 54, no. 9 (September 1963): 175.

A brief essay about neglect of church pianos.

*Tuner's Journal. See 34 under* General.

Turner, Earle M. "The Fundamentals of Piano Servicing." *See 441 under* Construction and Design—General Construction.

567. Waite, Roy. "The Care and Feeding of the Piano." *House Beautiful* 91, no. 8 (August 1949): 53, 97.

Discusses tuning, moth problems, moisture, cleaning, sympathetic vibrations, and cracked soundboard.

568. Weil, Alfred R. "Between the Keys (Care and Feeding)." *Piano Quarterly* 25, no. 97 (Spring 1977): 48.

A collection of anecdotes involving improper care and maintenance of pianos.

569. West, Richard E. *Notes on the Piano: Questions and Answers about Piano Care and Piano Buying.* [Lincoln, Nebr.: by the author, 1986.]

Primarily intended for piano owners. Topics include hammers, tuning, moving and placement of the piano, cleaning, repairing, purchasing, and voicing. Includes a list of suggested readings and a list of registered tuner-technicians in the Nebraska chapter of the Piano Technicians Guild in 1986. 25 pp.

570. White, William Braid. *Modern Piano Tuning and Allied Arts: Including Principles and Practice of Piano Tuning, Regulation of Piano Action, Repair of the Piano, Elementary Principles of Player-Piano Pneumatics, General Construction of Player Mechanisms, and Repair of Player Mechanism.* New York: Edward Lyman Bill, 1917.

Discusses tuning, maintenance and repair of pianos and player pianos. Topics include acoustics of the piano, temperament, tuning techniques, action regulation, voicing, and repairs specific to the player-piano mechanisms. Piano construction is addressed as it pertains to the above topics. Illustrations (many labeled). Bibliographical note. 341 pp.

571. ————. *Piano Tuning and Allied Arts.* 5th rev. and enl. ed. Boston: Tuners Supply Company, 1946. Reprint, Boston: Tuners Supply Company, 1948.

Discusses theory and procedures of tuning, tuning problems, temperament, general construction, voicing, and repairs. Appendix topics include raising the pitch and using the Conn Chromatic Stroboscope. Illustrations. Glossary, bibliography. 295 pp.

572. "Why a Piano Grows Old." *Music Teacher and Piano Student* 43, no. 5 (May 1964): 203.

Explains causes for deterioration of pianos and the effects of deterioration. Also discusses general construction.

573. Wicks, Don. *The Family Piano Doctor: A Step-by-Step Guide to the Repairing, Tuning and Renovating of the Family Piano.* London: B. T. Batsford, 1991.

A do-it-yourself guide to piano maintenance and repair. Discusses cleaning, action repairs, diagnosing problems, tuning, strings, regulating, toning, and casework renovation. Addresses uprights and grands. Includes a selective list of suppliers. Photographs, illustrations. 143 pp.

Willis, Aubrey. *Aubrey Willis Home Study Course in Piano Tuning and Repairing. See 443 under* Construction and Design—General Construction.

574. Winter, Robert [S.]. "The Most Unwitting Foes of the Romantic Piano May Be Those Well-Intentioned Curators Who Lend Their Instruments for Recording Sessions." *Early Music* 12, no. 1 (February 1984): 21–25.

Discusses problems in restoring and maintaining pianos built during the early to mid-nineteenth century.

Wolfenden, Samuel. *A Treatise on the Art of Pianoforte Construction. See 444 under* Construction and Design—General Construction.

575. Wood, Lawrence R[obert]. *Pianos, Anyone?* 1st ed. New York: Vantage Press, 1977.

An introduction to the selection and maintenance of the piano. Discusses purchasing, factors that affect the tuning and its stability, and other miscellaneous topics. Also answers some frequently asked questions about general maintenance. 48 pp.

576. Woodman, H. Staunton. *How to Tune a Piano, How to Clean Your Piano and Keep It in Good Condition, How to Buy a Used*

*Piano.* 2nd ed. Huntington, N.Y.: Corwood Publishers, 1963.

Originally published in 1960. Discusses theory and practice of tuning, temperament, construction, maintenance and care, troubleshooting, repairing, regulating, voicing, and purchasing a used or rebuilt piano. Illustrations (many labeled), tables. Bibliography. 67 pp.

577. Zalta, Edward N. "A Soft Touch." *Piano & Keyboard* no. 165 (November–December 1993): 13.

Discusses Edward J. McMorrow's Light Hammer Tone Regulation technique of action and tone regulation in which the piano is regulated as a whole.

# Action

578. Boone, Danny L. *Regulating Grand Piano Touch and Tone.* Waco, Tex.: Piano Technology Resources, 1993.

Detailed instructions for comprehensive regulation and voicing of the piano. Review questions are included at the end of each chapter. Appendices discuss minor repairs and tools needed for comprehesive regulation and include a checklist, a labeled Steinway grand action diagram, and a list of related articles in the *Piano Technicians Journal*, organized by topic. Photographs, illustrations. 207 pp.

Dietz, Franz Rudolf. *Das Regulieren von Flügeln bei Steinway* (The Regulation of the Steinway Grand Action). *See 471 under* Construction and Design—Action.

579. Durrenberger, Christopher. "The Instrument: Get into the Action." *Piano & Keyboard* no. 197 (March–April 1999): 14–17.

An introduction to evaluating the action. Discusses diagnosing and solving problems of the let-off, drop, backcheck, repetition spring, and aftertouch. Intended for performers, teachers, and students.

580. Esterowitz, Michael. "Piano Doctor." *Keyboard Classics* 2, no. 6 (November–December 1982): 14.

Discusses causes and repairs for sticking or sluggish keys. Illustration.

———. "Piano Doctor: Bad Action." *See 472 under* Construction and Design—Action.

581. ———. "Piano Doctor: Lost Motion." *Keyboard Classics* 4, no. 3 (May–June 1984): 47.

Discusses regulating the action with a focus on adjusting the capstans and the hammer blow distance. Also addresses some action problems.

582. ———. "Piano Doctor: Swollen Parts." *Keyboard Classics* 3, no. 1 (January–February 1983): 14.

Addresses sticking and sluggish keys. Discusses troubleshooting, causes, and repairs.

583. Fine, Larry. "The Weighting Game." *Piano & Keyboard* no. 163 (July–August 1993): 48–50.

A report on David Stanwood's computer-assisted procedure of weighting the action.

584. Kegley, Paul. "What Is Piano Touch?" *Music Journal* 27, no. 2 (February 1969): 32–33.

An introduction to action regulation with respect to the piano touch.

585. Kennedy, K. T. *Piano Action Repairs and Maintenance.* London: Kaye & Ward; South Brunswick, N.J.: A. S. Barnes and Company, 1979.

Instructions for repairing piano actions, addressing various parts of the actions of uprights and grands. Includes a metric conversion table. Illustrations (many labeled). 101 pp.

586. Kuerti, Anton. "Step by Step Guide for Determining If Your Piano Is in Good Regulation." *Clavier* 12, no. 5 (May–June 1973): 21–22.

    A twelve-point checklist for evaluating the grand piano regulation. Discusses special consideration for preparing the piano for concert performances.

587. Mason, Merle H., comp. *PTG Piano Action Handbook.* 2nd ed. With a foreword by James H. Burton. Seattle, Wash.: Piano Technicians Guild, 1971.

    In three sections. Section 1 explains the regulating dimensions for upright pianos, but also applicable to grands, through diagrams. Section 2 contains regulating dimension tables for pianos made in the United States, Canada, Europe, and Asia. Section 3 lists names and addresses of piano manufacturers in section 2. 55 pp.

588. "Music Trade Forum: Action Centres." *Musical Opinion* 89, no. 1059 (December 1965): 189; no. 1060 (January 1966): 253.

    Discusses action center problems and repairs (lubricating, rebushing, and repinning).

589. "Music Trade Forum: Action Regulating in a Grand Piano." *Musical Opinion* 83, no. 992 (May 1960): 589; no. 993 (June 1960): 653.

    Topics include causes for bad regulation and regulation procedures. Does not explain regulation of new instruments. Comparisons with upright pianos.

590. "Music Trade Forum: Clicking Keys." *Musical Opinion and Music Trade Review* 82, no. 983 (August 1959): 773.

    Discusses diagnosing problems associated with noises in keys. Primarily intended for non-technicians.

591. "Music Trade Forum: Double Escapement Regulation." *Musical Opinion* 84, no. 1001 (February 1961): 333.

Detailed instructions on regulating the set-off and the repetition mechanisms.

592. "Music Trade Forum: Felt and Centre-Pins." *Musical Opinion and Music Trade Review* 79, no. 948 (September 1956): 757.

Discusses action problems and repairs associated with worn felt or pins.

"Music Trade Forum: Grand Action Methods." *See 480 under* Construction and Design—Action.

593. "Music Trade Forum: Molineaux and Costa." *Musical Opinion and Music Trade Review* 74, no. 884 (May 1951): 441.

Addresses the problems and repairs of the spring and loop mechanism in the piano action.

594. "Music Trade Forum: Pianoforte Ironwork." *Musical Opinion and Music Trade Review* 80, no. 960 (September 1957): 773.

Discusses damaged pedals, broken action-standards in uprights, and bronzing cast-iron frames.

595. "Music Trade Forum: Piano Keys and Their Control." *Musical Opinion and Music Trade Review* 82, no. 981 (June 1959): 645.

An introductory article about factors that affect the regulation of the action. Based on *The Modern Piano* by Lawrence M. Nalder.

596. "Music Trade Forum: Regulation of Action in the Grand Piano." *Musical Opinion and Music Trade Review* 75, no. 889 (October 1951): 61; no. 890 (November 1951): 125; no. 891 (December 1951): 189.

A series of articles about issues and procedures of action regulating. Also briefly discusses damper regulation and voicing.

597. "Music Trade Forum: Setting Up the Action." *Musical Opinion*

*and Music Trade Review* 78, no. 930 (March 1955): 381; no. 931 (April 1955): 446.

Concerns the placement of the action in the piano case. Includes measurements. Based on *The Modern Piano* by Lawrence M. Nalder.

598. "Music Trade Forum: Smooth Touch." *Musical Opinion* 88, no. 1051 (April 1965): 445.

Addresses problems with upright actions and how to repair them. Discusses overdamper and underdamper actions.

599. "Music Trade Forum: Sticker Actions." *Musical Opinion and Music Trade Review* 81, no. 964 (January 1958): 293; no. 965 (February 1958): 358; no. 966 (March 1958): 429.

Instructions on cleaning and restoring older pianos that have sticker actions.

600. "Music Trade Forum: Stiff Piano Actions." *Musical Opinion and Music Trade Review* 79, no. 943 (April 1956): 445.

Discusses repairing action centers with problems due to extreme climate.

601. "Music Trade Forum: Tape Check Action Regulating." *Musical Opinion and Music Trade Review* 75, no. 892 (January 1952): 253; no. 893 (February 1952): 317.

Covers the upright piano actions and their regulation. Discusses overdamper and underdamper actions. Also discusses problems with dampers and pedals.

602. "Music Trade Forum: Touch." *Musical Opinion and Music Trade Review* 74, no. 882 (March 1951): 312.

Summarizes problems and procedures of action regulation.

603. "Music Trade Forum: Upright Piano Action Regulating." *Musical Opinion* 88, no. 1045 (October 1964): 61.

Explains procedures for regulating the upright action and related issues.

604. "Music Trade forum: 'Zithering' in Pianos." *Musical Opinion and Music Trade Review* 78, no. 929 (February 1956): 317.

Discusses bad checks when hammers rebound to the string as the note is played. Includes some suggestions for regulating the action.

605. Stanwood, David C. "New Touchweight Metrology." *Piano Technicians Journal* 39, no. 6 (June 1996): 16–18.

An introduction to the author's system of controlling the touchweight by measuring the effects of the weight of the action parts on the forces at the front of the keys. Includes terms and definitions. Photographs, illustrations.

606. ————. "Standard Protocols of the New Touchweight Metrology." *Piano Technicians Journal* 43, no. 2 (February 2000): 20–23.

Updates and standardizes an earlier article by the author, "New Touchweight Metrology," *Piano Technicians Journal* 39, no. 6 (June 1996): 16–18. Photographs, illustrations (labeled). Glossary.

607. "Striking a Balance: Piano Technician's Craft Wins Acclaim." *Boston Globe*, 24 February 1996, pp. 11, 14.

A report on the Stanwood system of action regulation. Brief description of the system, feedback from pianists and other technicians, and Stanwood's biographical background. Photograph.

608. Stuart, Wayne D. *Theory and Practice of Pianoforte Action Regulation.* Sydney: by the author, 1978.

Intended for piano technicians. A detailed guide on regulating grands and uprights. Illustrations. 136 pp.

609. Tasciotti, Lou. "The Technician's View: The Well-Regulated

Grand Piano." *Piano Quarterly* 39, no. 154 (Summer 1991): 45–46, 48.

A description of a piano that is in good regulation and how to check it.

610. Ten Dyke, Richard. "The Right Touch: Happiness Is Restoring an Old Piano . . . Correctly." *Keyboard Classics & Piano Stylist* 14, no. 1 (January–February 1994): 12, 63.

Discusses the Stanwood system of action regulation and its use in restoring pianos. Photographs.

611. Tittle, Martin B. "Amplifying the Kenzoid: Part 2—Regulation." *Piano Quarterly* 26, no. 103 (Fall 1978): 24–27.

Explains the procedures and effects of action regulation. Includes a brief discussion about the construction of the action. Photographs.

Wilson, Chas West. "Instructions for Adjusting the English Piano Action." *See 185 under* History—England.

## Case and Frame

612. "Music Trade Forum: Case-Work." *Musical Opinion and Music Trade Review* 74, no. 888 (September 1951): 681.

Discusses fixing the hinges to the lid of a new or used grand piano.

"Music Trade Forum: Continental Finish." *See 488 under* Construction and Design—Case and Frame.

613. "Music Trade Forum: Damaged Veneering." *Musical Opinion and Music Trade Review* 82, no. 982 (July 1959): 709.

Discusses repairing blistered veneers in the case caused by excessive heat or moisture applied accidentally to the instrument.

"Music Trade Forum: French Polishing." *See 489 under* Construction and Design—Case and Frame.

614. "Music Trade Forum: Piano Finish." *Musical Opinion and Music Trade Review* 75, no. 894 (March 1952): 381; no. 895 (April 1952): 445; no. 896 (May 1952): 509; no. 897 (June 1952): 573.

Discusses piano case refinishing. Addresses French polishing, varnishing, and lacquering. [Note: This is different from the article by the same title in vol. 85, no. 1020 (September 1962).]

"Music Trade Forum: Pianoforte Ironwork." *See 594 under* Maintenance and Repair—Action.

"Music Trade Forum: The Convenience of French Polishing." *See 490 under* Construction and Design—Case and Frame.

"Music Trade Forum: The Decline of French Polishing." *See 491 under* Construction and Design—Case and Frame.

"Music Trade Forum: The Iron Frame and the Strings." *See 424 under* Construction and Design—General Construction.

"Music Trade Forum: The Three Methods of Polishing." *See 493 under* Construction and Design—Case and Frame.

# Cleaning

615. Esterowitz, Michael. "Piano Doctor: Keep It Clean!" *Keyboard Classics* 4, no. 4 (July–August 1984): 48.

Instructions on cleaning the soundboard. Also discusses cleaning the damper heads.

616. "Music Trade Forum: Interior Appearance of the Piano." *Musical Opinion* 84, no. 1000 (January 1961): 269.

Addresses removing rust from the interior of the piano (strings, bolts, and hammer felts).

617. "Music Trade Forum: The Modern Piano: Interior Cleaning." *Musical Opinion and Music Trade Review* 80, no. 956 (May 1957): 509.

 Discusses cleaning procedures for both grands and uprights. Includes comments specific to some brands.

## Climate Control

618. "Allen Foote Creates Complete 'Climate Control System.'" *Music Trades* 119, no. 2 (February 1971): 45–46.

 Discusses Allen M. Foote, president and founder of Dampp-Chaser Electronics, and his invention Piano Climate Control System used for controlling humidity as well as dryness. Photographs.

619. Campbell, Denele [Pitts]. "Humidity Is the Enemy." *Clavier* 37, no. 5 (May–June 1998): 26–28.

 Discusses basic care of the piano, particularly humidity.

620. Fine, Larry. "The Piano Technician: 'Tis the Season to Be Tuning." *Keyboard* 12, no. 10 (October 1986): 109.

 Discusses the effect of climate on tuning and the time for tuning (with seasonal considerations). Illustration.

621. Malone, Thomas. "Of Pianos, Heat, and Humidity." *Clavier* 34, no. 5 (May–June 1995): 26–27.

 An essay about climate control and the effects of humidity on the piano. Photographs.

622. "Music Trade Forum: Seasonal Changes in Piano Pitch." *Musical Opinion and Music Trade Review* 81, no. 963 (December 1957): 221.

 Discusses the effect of the climate on piano strings. Focuses on changes in pitch due to expansion and contraction of the strings. Also discusses tuning stability and string breakages.

623. "Music Trade Forum: Summer Madness." *Musical Opinion and Music Trade Review* 79, no. 946 (July 1956): 637.

Explains the effect of the climate on the piano and its tuning.

624. "Music Trade Forum: The Air Which Your Piano Breathes." *Musical Opinion* 84, no. 1008 (September 1961): 781.

Discusses climate control and the effects of the climate on the piano. Addresses problems with central heating.

625. "Music Trade Forum: The Commonest Fault." *Musical Opinion and Music Trade Review* 79, no. 942 (March 1956): 381.

Addresses issues concerning climate control, especially humidity control. Some information contained in the article is outdated.

626. "Piano Out of Tune?" *School Musician Director and Teacher* 39, no. 7 (March 1968): 68.

A short article about dryness and piano tuning.

627. Tasciotti, Lou. "Tuning: Part I—Climate Control and Stabilizing Pitch." *Piano Quarterly* 37, no. 145 (Spring 1989): 40–42.

Discusses tuning instability attributed to the technician, climate control, and seasonal effects. Continued in "The Technician's View: Tuning, Part 2—'A Good, Solid Tuning,'" in *Piano Quarterly* 37, no. 146 (Summer 1989): 52–55.

628. "Veteran Piano-Violin Teacher Tames 'Wild' Piano." *Music Trades* 122, no. 3 (March 1974): 100–101.

A short article about Dampp-Chaser's Humidity Control System and the effect of humidity on the piano. The text is reprinted as "Vet Tames Wild Piano" in *Music Journal* 32, no. 9 (November 1974): 6. Photographs.

## Dampers

629. "Music Trade Forum: Dampers." *Musical Opinion and Music Trade Review* 79, no. 945 (June 1956): 573.

    Discusses damper problems and repairs for grands and uprights.

"Music Trade Forum: Dampers." *See 496 under* Construction and Design—Dampers.

## Hammers

Boone, Danny L. *Regulating Grand Piano Touch and Tone. See 578 under* Maintenance and Repair—Action.

630. Cloutier, Robert. "A Tip for the Top." *Piano & Keyboard* no. 188 (September–October 1997): 23.

    Gives advice on hammer work to get a clear sustaining treble sound in Steinways. Photograph.

631. Dietz, Franz Rudolf. *Das Intonieren von Flügeln* (Grand Voicing). Fachbuchreihe Das Musikinstrument, vol. 20. Frankfurt am Main: Das Musikinstrument, 1968.

    Topics include needling, filing, preparation and procedures for voicing, and voicing in the "shift position." In German, English, French, Swedish, and Italian. English text on pp. 19–26. German and English texts have been reprinted by American Piano Supply Co. (Clifton, N.J.). Sixteen photographs. 55 pp.

632. Esterowitz, Michael. "Minor Surgery." *Keyboard Classics* 3, no. 3 (May–June 1983): 41.

    Discusses obvious problems such as broken strings and broken hammer shanks, and their repairs. Illustration.

633. Fine, Larry. "The Piano Technician: Changing Tone, Part I: Strings & Hammers." *Keyboard* 14, no. 3 (March 1988): 128.

Addresses the condition of strings and hammers as they relate to the piano tone. Discusses cleaning the strings and filing the hammers. Illustration.

634. ————. "The Piano Technician: Changing Tone, Part II: Voicing." *Keyboard* 14, no. 4 (April 1988): 125.

Discusses preparation for voicing (needling and hardening). Includes some tips on working with a technician.

635. ————. "The Piano Technician: How to Glue a Broken Hammer Shank." *Keyboard* 13, no. 7 (July 1987): 140.

Do-it-yourself instructions for minor repairs of broken hammer shanks. Illustrations.

636. Gatz, P. W. "You and Your Piano: Tone Regulation." *Music Journal* 11, no. 9 (September 1953): 56–57.

Addresses factors that affect the piano tone. Discusses hammers and voicing.

637. Little, J. W. *Toning.* N.p.: Institute of Musical Instrument Technology, [1963].

Discusses voicing procedures, especially needling. Topics include hammer felts, deep and surface voicing, and ironing. "A talk given at Beale's Restaurant after the dinner on Tuesday, November 26th, 1963." Includes a transcription of the question-and-answer session after the talk. Photographs, illustrations. 16 pp.

638. Mohn, Norman Carroll. "Voicing, a 'Sound' Investment." *Piano Teacher* 8, no. 1 (September–October 1965): 14–15.

A nontechnical introduction to voicing procedures. Discusses filing, needling, and unacceptable voicing practices.

639. "Music Trade Forum: Piano Hammers." *Musical Opinion and Music Trade Review* 78, no. 926 (November 1954): 125.

Instructions for replacing the felt covering on piano hammers.

640. "Music Trade Forum: Piano Toning." *Musical Opinion and Music Trade Review* 82, no. 979 (April 1959): 501.

Explains factors that affect the piano tone. Discusses voicing (filing and needling).

641. "Music Trade Forum: Toning." *Musical Opinion and Music Trade Review* 74, no. 877 (October 1950): 59; no. 879 (November–December 1950): 122.

Discusses the relationship between hammer-felt quality and tone. Also discusses voicing newly re-covered hammers. Focuses on needling.

642. "Music Trade Forum: Toning the Hammers." *Musical Opinion* 84, no. 1002 (March 1961): 397.

Explains voicing procedures and reasons for voicing. Discusses filing and needling.

643. "Music Trade Forum: Wear in Piano Hammers." *Musical Opinion and Music Trade Review* 81, no. 962 (November 1957): 141.

Discusses filing and factors that cause unusual wear of hammers.

644. Porter, Thomas. "Voicing: A Pianist's Guide to the Care of Hammers." *Clavier* 7, no. 5 (May–June 1968): 12–17.

Explains the procedures and effects of voicing. Photographs, illustrations.

645. Stokes, A. W. "The 'Life' of Fine Tone in a Piano." *Music Teacher and Piano Student* 31, no. 3 (March 1952): 134.

Addresses deterioration in pianos and its effect on the tone. Discusses soundboards and hammers.

646. Stuart, Wayne D. *Theory and Practice of Pianoforte Voicing.* Sydney: by the author, 1977.

Intended for piano technicians. Discusses the soundboard and its effect on the tone, new hammers, voicing old or used hammers, posture, tools and equipment, string adjustment, regulation, striking line, repair, needling, filing, ironing, seasoning and second voicing. Photographs, illustrations. 32 pp.

647. Tasciotti, Lou. "The Technician's View: Voicing—The Great Controversy." *Piano Quarterly* 38, no. 150 (Summer 1990): 51–54.

Covers procedures and effects of voicing. Discusses filing and the controversies surrounding needling and lacquering. Includes a description of a well-voiced piano.

648. Tittle, Martin [B.]. "Amplifying the Kenzoid: Part 3—Voicing." *Piano Quarterly* 27, no. 106 (Summer 1979): 42–47.

Discusses the purpose, effect, and procedures of voicing. Also discusses the hammer construction and the string behavior upon impact with the hammer. Photographs, illustrations.

# Keys

649. "Music Trade Forum: Keys and Their Covering." *Musical Opinion and Music Trade Review* 81, no. 970 (July 1958): 685.

Discusses making and repairing keys with ivory key covering.

650. "Music Trade Forum: Piano Key Bushing." *Musical Opinion and Music Trade Review* 82, no. 984 (September 1959): 845.

Addresses problems associated with wear in bushings. Discusses repairs of minor wear and replacement of worn-out bushings.

651. "Music Trade Forum: Piano Key Levers: Repair and Regulation." *Musical Opinion and Music Trade Review* 83, no. 985 (October 1959): 69.

Discusses the final regulation of the keyboard and difficulties commonly encountered.

652. "Music Trade Forum: Re-Covering Worn Keys." *Musical Opinion and Music Trade Review* 81, no. 971 (August 1958): 749.

     Discusses servicing ivory key coverings. Topics include replacing worn-out covers and cleaning discolored covers.

653. "Music Trade Forum: Repinning Keys." *Musical Opinion and Music Trade Review* 76, no. 910 (July 1953): 637.

     Discusses replacing the pins in the key frame.

## Pedals

654. Esterowitz, Michael. "Piano Doctor: Grand Pedal Problems." *Keyboard Classics* 3, no. 5 (September–October 1983): 39.

     Discusses troubleshooting and minor repairs, including removal and gluing of lyres.

655. ———. "Piano Doctor: Squeaks and Groans!" *Keyboard Classics* 3, no. 4 (July–August 1983): 39.

     Discusses squeaking or creaking damper pedals and their repair. Illustration.

656. Fine, Larry. "The Piano Technician: Pedal Adjustments of the Rich and Famous." *Keyboard* 13, no. 5 (May 1987): 112.

     Discusses minor adjustment and repair of the pedals, with a focus on the damper pedal. Illustrations.

"Music Trade Forum: Pianoforte Ironwork." *See 594 under* Maintenance and Repair—Action.

"Music Trade Forum: The Middle Pedal." *See 506 under* Construction and Design—Pedals.

## Rebuilding and Restoration

657. Donelson, James H., comp. *Piano Rebuilders' Handbook of Treble String Tensions (and Other Characteristics)*. Pleasant Hill, Calif.: by the author, 1977.

Tables of string tensions from note 21 to note 88, primarily for a rebuilder who needs to improve the scale on pianos with poor original design. The foreword includes some suggestions in rescaling a piano. Illustrations. 650 pp., unpaginated.

658. Field, Werner. *How to Redecorate Your Old Piano . . . and Make It Look Great!* [Medford, Ore.]: Shinn Music Aids, 1972.

Explains how to replace the case and keytops of upright pianos. Intended for nonprofessionals with or without musical training. Photographs, illustrations. Includes a short bibliography. 44 pp.

659. Kehret, Peg. *Refinishing & Restoring Your Piano*. Blue Ridge Summit, Pa.: Tab Books, 1985.

Addresses the merits of refinishing and/or restoring an old piano rather than purchasing a new piano, selecting an old piano for refinishing or restoring, and the procedures of refinishing and restoring. The appendix lists suppliers. Photographs, illustrations (many labeled). 119 pp.

660. Latcham, Michael. "Soundboards Old & New." *Galpin Society Journal* no. 45 (March 1992): 50–58.

Discusses repairing and replacing soundboards in early pianos. Special comments about Viennese pianos.

661. "Music Trade Forum: Fundamentals of Piano Renovation." *Musical Opinion and Music Trade Review* 76, no. 912 (September 1953): 757.

An overview of piano restoration procedures.

662. Tasciotti, Lou. "Sound Decisions: Will Rebuilding Your Piano

Give You the Sound You Want?" *Piano & Keyboard* no. 174 (May–June 1995): 24–29.

An overview of the process and merits of rebuilding a piano, with a focus on Steinway pianos. Photographs.

663. ———. "The Technician's View: Piano Rebuilding." *Piano Quarterly* 39, no. 152 (Winter 1990–1991): 58–60.

Addresses confusion surrounding the term "rebuilding," issues in rebuilding a piano, and the rebuilding process.

Ten Dyke, Richard. "The Right Touch: Happiness Is Restoring an Old Piano . . . Correctly." *See 610 under* Maintenance and Repair—Action.

664. Usher, Terence. "Square Pianos." *Galpin Society Journal* no. 13 (July 1960): 92–93.

A brief article about the author's method of restoring square pianos with single, rather than double, stringing.

665. Watson, John. "Three Examples of Keyboard Restoration in the Southeast." *Early Keyboard Journal* 1 (1982–83): 16–24.

Descriptions of restoration work done on a spinet by Charles Haward (c. 1685), a square piano by Johannes Pohlman (1769), and a square piano by John Watson (c. 1797; the name is an apparent coincidence). Discusses issues in restoring rare and historical instruments.

666. Winston, David. "Other Voices, Other Rooms: An Instrument Tells Its Own Story." *Piano Quarterly* 40, no. 159 (Fall 1992): 40–42.

An essay about the author's restoration of Beethoven's 1817 Broadwood grand piano.

667. ———. "The Restoration of Beethoven's 1817 Broadwood Grand Piano." *Galpin Society Journal* no. 46 (March 1993): 147–51.

Discusses the author's restoration of Beethoven's 1817 Broadwood grand piano.

## Soundboard

Esterowitz, Michael. "The Piano Doctor: Is Your Soundboard Healthy?" *See 508 under* Construction and Design—Soundboard.

Latcham, Michael. "Soundboards Old & New." *See 660 under* Maintenance and Repair—Rebuilding and Restoration.

Stokes, A. W. "The 'Life' of Fine Tone in a Piano." *See 645 under* Maintenance and Repair—Hammers.

Stuart, Wayne D. *Theory and Practice of Pianoforte Voicing. See 646 under* Maintenance and Repair—Hammers.

## Strings

Donelson, James H., comp. *Piano Rebuilders' Handbook of Treble String Tensions (and Other Characteristics). See 657 under* Maintenance and Repair—Rebuilding and Restoration.

Esterowitz, Michael. "Minor Surgery." *See 632 under* Maintenance and Repair—Hammers.

Fine, Larry. "The Piano Technician: Changing Tone, Part I: Strings & Hammers." *See 633 under* Maintenance and Repair—Hammers.

668. "Music Trade Forum: About Bass Strings." *Musical Opinion* 88, no. 1056 (September 1965): 769.

Discusses repairing broken bass strings. Includes some general comments about restringing. Illustrations.

669. "Music Trade Forum: Restringing the Pianoforte." *Musical Opinion* 83, no. 995 (August 1960): 781.

Discusses factors that contribute to the deterioration of the strings, how to detect faulty strings, and steps for restringing.

"Music Trade Forum: Seasonal Changes in Piano Pitch." *See 622 under* Maintenance and Repair—Climate Control.

670. "Music Trade Forum: Stringing." *Musical Opinion and Music Trade Review* 73, no. 875 (August 1950): 676; no. 876 (September 1950): 741.

Discusses restringing procedures, from removing the strings to the final tuning. Addresses differences between uprights and grands.

"Music Trade Forum: The Iron Frame and the Strings." *See 424 under* Construction and Design—General Construction.

671. Travis, John W. *How to Restring a Grand Piano*. Chicago: Schaff Piano Supply Company, 1955.

Step-by-step instructions on restringing, from assembling the tools and supplies to setting the bearing and lowering the plate. Intended primarily for piano technicians. Tables. 16 pp.

672. ———. *A Guide to Restringing*. 2nd ed. Edited by Michael R. Travis. With a foreword by Wendell E. Eaton. Takoma Park, Md.: by the author, 1982.

Originally published in 1961. In two parts. Part 1 discusses general procedures, scales, installation and removal of a pinblock, repairs of soundboard, agraffes, bridges, and tuning. Part 2 contains tables of scales by piano manufacturer and model. Photographs, tables, illustrations. 508 pp.

# Tools and Supplies

673. Fine, Larry. "The Piano Technician: A Tool Box for the Working Pianist." *Keyboard* 13, no. 3 (March 1987): 118.

Discusses tools pianists should have for basic maintenance of the piano. Illustration.

674. "Music Trade Forum: About Modern Adhesives." *Musical Opinion* 87, no. 1040 (May 1964): 509.

Discusses synthetic adhesive resins and their advantages, particularly the Aerolite resin glue.

675. "Music Trade Forum: Making a Pin Remover." *Musical Opinion and Music Trade Review* 79, no. 947 (August 1956): 693.

Instructions on making a tool for removing center pins from the action. Illustrations (labeled).

676. "Music Trade Forum: Tool Kit and Specials." *Musical Opinion* 88, no. 1055 (August 1965): 705.

Discusses tools and supplies needed for tuning and minor repairs of the piano.

## Tuning

677. Beatey, Robert W. *Secrets of Piano Tuning: A Simple, Progressive Method of Piano Tuning That Can Be Properly Executed by Following Twenty Easy Steps.* N.p.: by the author, 1955.

A practical guide to tuning. Includes a glossary and background information about the theory of tuning. Also discusses old pianos and tuning the piano to lower pitch. 12 pp.

Colbert, Warren E. *Piano Tuning for Piano Player*s. *See 530 under* Maintenance and Repair—General Maintenance and Repair.

678. Crowder, Louis. "Electronic Piano Tuning." *Piano Quarterly* 34, no. 132 (Winter 1985–1986): 50–56.

Discusses electronically-assisted piano tuning. Topics include types of tuning devices and problems in using the tuning hammer. A list of suggested reading materials.

679. Dyer, Daniel L. *How to Tune a Piano in One Hour—Electronically.* Bronxville, N.Y.: by the author, 1975.

> Discusses using the Tunemaster, an electronic tuning device. For readers familiar with the vocabulary and the basic ideas of tuning. Photographs. 25 pp.

680. Feaster, C. Raymond. *The Dynamic Scale and How to Tune It.* Louisville, Ky.: by the author, 1958.

> Discusses tuning with a slight departure from the strict equal temperament. Includes some elementary acoustical information. The appendix addresses pitch raising of a half tone or more. Photographs. 47 pp.

681. Fine, Larry. "The Piano Technician: A Layman's Guide to Tuning Pianos." *Keyboard* 13, no. 2 (February 1987): 125.

> Do-it-yourself instructions on touch-up tuning (tuning unisons). Illustration.

———. "The Piano Technician: 'Tis the Season to Be Tuning." *See 620 under* Maintenance and Repair—Climate Control.

682. ———. "The Piano Technician: Tuning, Part I: Slippin' and Slidin' around the Pins." *Keyboard* 12, no. 9 (September 1986): 128.

> Discusses conditions that affect tuning stability. Illustration.

Fischer, J[erry]. Cree. *Piano Tuning: A Simple and Accurate Method for Amateurs. See 409 under* Construction and Design—General Construction.

Funke, Otto. *The Piano and How to Care for It: Piano Tuning in Theory and Practice. See 410 under* Construction and Design—General Construction.

683. Gatz, P. W. "You and Your Piano: Tuning." *Music Journal* 11, no. 7 (July 1953): 24; no. 8 (August 1953): 32.

Topics include the history of tuning and temperament, factors that affect the tuning, and possible causes for instability of tuning.

684. Hardin, Donald C. *A New Method for Electric Piano Tuning.* Stockton, Calif.: Hardin Piano Service, 1982.

Step-by-step instructions on using Hale Sight-O-Tuner. 15 pp., plus tables.

685. Harlow, Lewis A. "How to Tune Your Own Piano?" *Music Journal* 27, no. 3 (March 1969): 42, 71, 73–74.

Explains procedures for touch-up tuning. Discusses tuning unisons and octaves. Photographs.

686. Howell, W[alter] Dean. *Professional Piano Tuning.* 2nd ed. Clifton, N.J.: American Piano Supply, 1969.

A practical guide to tuning. Topics include factors that affect the tuning, inharmonicity, tools, pitch raising and lowering, and final checking. Covers left-hand and right-hand tuning. The appendix includes notes from annual conventions of the Piano Technicians Guild, an article by the author, and an interview with the author, reprinted from *Piano Technicians Journal.* Photographs, illustrations. 136 pp.

Jackson, Jim. *Tuning & Repairing Your Own Piano. See 542 under* Maintenance and Repair—General Maintenance and Repair.

Johnson, Michael, and Robin Mackworth-Young. *Tune and Repair Your Own Piano: A Practical and Theoretical Guide to the Tuning of All Keyboard Stringed Instruments, and to the Running Repair of the Piano. See 543 under* Maintenance and Repair—General Maintenance and Repair.

687. Kegley, Paul. "Problems of Piano Tuning." *Music Journal* 26, no. 1 (January 1968): 60–61.

An introductory essay about tuning. Discusses reasons for tuning, frequency of tuning, and the importance of tuning to A-440.

688. Mack, Albert. "Learn to Tune Your Piano." *Clavier* 3, no. 4 (September 1964): 24–26.

An introduction to basic tuning skills and procedures. Discusses tuning unisons and octaves. Includes a table of step-by-step procedures for tuning all notes of the octave. Photographs.

689. Moore, Arthur. "Tuning a Keyboard: A New Solution." *Musical Times* 99, no. 1389 (November 1958): 606.

Introduces a tuning scheme devised by the author who claims that the scheme results in a brighter sound.

690. "Music Trade Forum: An Alternative Method of Tuning." *Musical Opinion and Music Trade Review* 80, no. 950 (November 1956): 125.

Presents a scheme in which the piano is tuned by thirds and sixths rather than by fourths and fifths.

691. "Music Trade Forum: Beats and Boredom." *Musical Opinion* 85, no. 1017 (July 1962): 637.

Summarizes different tuning schemes.

692. "Music Trade Forum: Efficiency in Tuning." *Musical Opinion* 86, no. 1022 (November 1962): 125.

Presents a different tuning scheme to avoid boredom and fatigue.

693. "Music Trade Forum: Getting Your Bearings." *Musical Opinion* 83, no. 991 (April 1960): 517.

A summary of various schemes for laying a tempered scale.

694. "Music Trade Forum: Laying the Bearing." *Musical Opinion and Music Trade Review* 75, no. 898 (July 1952): 637; 75, no. 899 (August 1952): 701; 75, no. 900 (September 1952): 765; 76, no. 901 (October 1952): 61.

Discusses the history, theory, and procedures of tuning and

tempering. Presents two tempering schemes.

695. "Music Trade Forum: Loose Tuning Pins." *Musical Opinion* 87, no. 1037 (February 1964): 317.

Discusses causes of loose tuning pins such as poor hammer technique.

696. "Music Trade Forum: Theory and Practice in Piano Tuning." *Musical Opinion and Music Trade Review* 83, no. 988 (January 1960): 301.

Explains equal temperament and tuning. Also discusses inharmonicity.

697. "Music Trade Forum: Tuning a Pianoforte without Wedges." *Musical Opinion and Music Trade Review* 77, no. 924 (September 1954): 741.

Discusses how to tune minipianos and other pianos where inserting a tuning wedge is difficult and risky.

698. "Music Trade Forum: Tuning in Unison and at the Octave." *Musical Opinion and Music Trade Review* 76, no. 902 (November 1952): 125.

Instructions for tuning the whole keyboard after the middle octave has been tuned and tempered.

699. Nalder, Lawrence M[arcus]. *First Steps in Piano Tuning and Other Essays in Pianoforte Technology*. London: Musical Opinion, 1939.

An introduction to piano tuning. Other articles discuss fine tuning, setting the pin, tools and equipment, tuning in the presence of distractions, and selecting and purchasing a piano. Illustrations. 80 pp.

700. "Piano Tuning with a Precision Metronome." *Musik international—Instrumentenbau-Zeitschrift* 37, no. 10 (October 1983): 636–37.

Discusses tuning with a metronome that has a precision bar indicator.

Rasch, Rudolf A., and Vincent Heetvelt. "String Inharmonicity and Piano Tuning." *See 466 under* Construction and Design—Acoustics.

701. Richards, James D. "The Piano: Some Factors Affecting Tuning Stability." *American Music Teacher* 28, no. 6 (June–July 1979): 16–19.

Discusses the history of tuning and tuning stability. Illustrations (labeled).

Rosencrantz, I[sidor] B[ertram]. *The Piano: Its Construction, and Relation to Tone, Pitch and Temperament, with Directions How to Use the "Tunella" in Conjunction with the Piano, to Learn the Art of Piano Tuning. See 435 under* Construction and Design—General Construction.

702. Seybold, A. M. "An All-Electronic Method for Tuning Organs and Pianos." *Audio* 47, no. 2 (February 1963): 28–32, 59–61; 47, no. 5 (May 1963): 20–24; 48, no. 3 (March 1964): 22–24, 72–73.

Addresses the use of an electronic tuning device. General procedure and step-by-step instructions. Discusses American and international standards, use of a tuning oscillator, tuning accuracy, and standard and nonstandard frequencies. Photograph, illustrations, tables.

703. Stevens, Floyd A. *Complete Course in Electronic Piano Tuning.* Professional/Technical Series. Chicago: Nelson-Hall Company, 1974.

Discusses the construction of the piano and tuning, particularly with the aid of an electronic tuning device. Detailed instructions on tuning (by make and model of the tuning device). Also discusses selection and advantages of using a tuning device, as well as business tips. Photographs, illustrations. 257 pp.

704. Swackhamer, William. "Do Your Own Corrective Piano Tuning." *Instrumentalist* 23, no. 10 (May 1969): 28.

Instructions on touch-up tuning between professional tunings.

Tasciotti, Lou. "Tuning: Part I—Climate Control and Stabilizing Pitch." *See 627 under* Maintenance and Repair—Climate Control.

705. ———. "The Technician's View: Tuning, Part 2—'A Good, Solid Tuning.'" *Piano Quarterly* 37, no. 146 (Summer 1989): 52–55.

Continued from his "Tuning: Part I—Climate Control and Stabilizing Pitch," in *Piano Quarterly* 37, no. 145 (Spring 1989): 40–42. Discusses tuning stability and octave stretching.

706. Tittle, Martin B. "Amplifying the Kenzoid: Part 1–Tuning." *Piano Quarterly* 26, no. 102 (Summer 1978): 41–45.

Discusses the procedures, effects, and limitations of tuning. Includes a brief history of tuning and temperament. Illustration.

707. Weinreich, Gabriel. "The Coupled Motions of Piano Strings." *Scientific American* 240, no. 1 (January 1979): 118–27.

Discusses the tuning of unisons and their effect on the piano sound. Includes an overview of the construction of the piano and the action. Illustrations.

White, William Braid. *Modern Piano Tuning and Allied Arts: Including Principles and Practice of Piano Tuning, Regulation of Piano Action, Repair of the Piano, Elementary Principles of Player-Piano Pneumatics, General Construction of Player Mechanisms, and Repair of Player Mechanism. See 570 under* Maintenance and Repair—General Maintenance and Repair.

———. *Piano Tuning and Allied Arts. See 571 under* Maintenance and Repair—General Maintenance and Repair.

———. *Theory and Practice of Piano Construction: With a Detailed, Practical Method for Tuning. See 442 under* Construction and

Design—General Construction.

Woodman, H. Staunton. *How to Tune a Piano, How to Clean Your Piano and Keep It in Good Condition, How to Buy a Used Piano. See 576 under* Maintenance and Repair—General Maintenance and Repair.

## Wrest Plank

708. "Music Trade Forum: Fitting a New Wrestplank." *Musical Opinion* 84, no. 997 (October 1960): 69.

    Discusses cracked or split wrest planks and procedures for replacing them.

709. "Music Trade Forum: More about Wrestplanks." *Musical Opinion* 84, no. 998 (November 1960): 133.

    Addresses wrest plank problems caused by the tuning pins.

710. "Music Trade Forum: The Wrest Plank." *Musical Opinion and Music Trade Review* 74, no. 885 (June 1951): 505; no. 886 (July 1951): 561; no. 887 (August 1951): 617.

    Addresses problems and repairs of the wrest plank. Discusses cracked wood, faulty gluing (especially in older pianos), and replacing the wrest plank. Includes a list of references on adhesives, and a short comment about fitting hinges of a grand piano lid.

711. "Music Trade Forum: Wrest Pins." *Musical Opinion and Music Trade Review* 74, no. 880 (January 1951): 185.

    Addresses problems with tuning pins, particularly with regard to the wrest plank.

712. "Music Trade Forum: Wrestplank Difficulties." *Musical Opinion* 83, no. 996 (September 1960): 853.

    Discusses worn-out pin holes and unglued wrest planks.

## Miscellaneous

713. Brady, Thomas M. "Are You Prepared for the Prepared Piano?" *Clavier* 18, no. 3 (March 1979): 58.

Discusses possible damage to a piano caused by the "prepared" piano. Includes comments from some manufacturers on the effect of "preparing" on the warranties.

714. Bunger, Richard. *The Well-Prepared Piano*. With a foreword by John Cage. 2nd American ed. San Pedro, Calif.: Litoral Arts Press, 1981.

Explains proper preparation for "prepared piano" works. The introductory chapters are questions and answers on how to minimize damage from the preparation and an overview of the piano construction. 94 pp.

715. Hill, N. E. "Moving the Piano." *Making Music* no. 46 (Summer 1961): 10.

Discusses precautions to be taken when moving the piano. Also addresses some basic maintenance.

716. "Music Trade Forum: The Modern Piano: Treatment of Pests." *Musical Opinion and Music Trade Review* 80, no. 957 (June 1957): 573.

Discusses pest control inside and around the piano.

# Miscellaneous

## Catalogs for Collections and Exhibits

717. Boomkamp, C[arel] van Leeuwen, and J. H. van der Meer. *The Carel van Leeuwen Boomkamp Collection of Musical Instruments*. Amsterdam: Frits Knuf, 1971.

A descriptive catalog of the early musical instruments in the collection. Dates of the pianos, physical descriptions with measurements, notes about the action and other features of the construction, and a brief biographical sketch of the builders. Photographs. 188 pp.

718. Cambridge Pianoforte Services. *The History of the Pianoforte: An Exhibition at St. Michael's Hall, Trinity Street, Cambridge, 25th–29th June 1985, 10 a.m.–6.30 p.m., to Be Held in Aid of the Music Therapy Department of Fulbourn Hospital, Cambridge*. Cambridge, England: Cambridge Pianoforte Services, [1985].

A descriptive catalog of instruments at the exhibit. An entry may contain a physical description and information about dates, builder, serial numbers, a photograph, and other pertinent background information. The thirty-seven instruments include grands, squares, verticals, reproducing pianos, and other unusual pianos. 24 pp.

719. *Catalogue of Musical Instruments, Principally Illustrative of the History of the Pianoforte: The Property of Henry Boddington, Pownall Hall, Wilmslow, Formerly the Collection of J. Kendrick Pyne, Organist of Manchester Cathedral and Town Hall*. Man-

chester, England: G. Falkner & Sons, 1888.

The collection contains fifty-eight instruments, thirty-one of which are western keyboard instruments (nineteen pianos). An entry may include an illustration of the instrument and information about the compass, dates and the origin, the builder, inscription (if any), important features, and prior ownership, in addition to pertinent general historical information about the instrument type. 86 leaves, unpaginated.

720. Colt, C. F., and Anthony Miall. *The Early Piano*. London: Stainer & Bell, 1981.

Describes the early pianos in C. F. Colt's collection. Physical description, some details of construction, and a color photograph for each of the thirty-six featured instruments (including two harpsichords). Also includes an overview of the history of the piano, performance suggestions, and discussions on maintaining and dating early pianos. Photographs, illustrations. Glossary. 160 pp.

721. Cselenyi, Ladislav. *Musical Instruments in the Royal Ontario Museum*. With a foreword by H. Hickl-Szabo. Toronto: Royal Ontario Museum, 1971.

A catalog of historical instruments at the museum, dating from the late sixteenth to the nineteenth century. Photograph and description (dates, origin, serial number, inscriptions, construction, size) of each instrument. Includes four pianos: two squares, one grand, and one upright. Bibliography. 96 pp.

Engel, Carl. *A Descriptive Catalogue of the Musical Instruments in the South Kensington Museum, Preceded by an Essay on the History of Musical Instruments. See 61 under* History—General History.

722. Gleich, Clemens von, ed. *Checklist of Pianos: Musical Instrument Collection, Haags Gemeentemuseum*. With a preface by Rob van Acht. Checklist of the Musical Instrument Collection of the Haags Gemeentemuseum, The Hague, vol. 1. The Hague, The Netherlands: Haags Gemeentemuseum, 1986.

A catalog of the seventy-six pianos at the museum. Includes

grands, uprights, squares, upright grands, cabinet pianos, practice keyboards, and other unusual pianos. Each entry may contain photographs of the instrument, information about the date, origin of the instrument, builder, nameboard, inscription, serial number, dimensions, and general constructional features (stringing, string lengths, actions, pedals, keys, etc.), as well as restoration information, literature references, and the museum catalog number. Bibliography, list of terms in four languages (English, Dutch, German, and French), a short discography. 119 pp.

———. *Pianofortes uit de Lage Landen* (Pianofortes from the Low Countries). *See 191 under* History—The Netherlands.

Hollis, Helen R[ice]. *The Pianos in the Smithsonian Institution. See 95 under* History—General History.

723. Kelly, Rodger S. "A Catalog of European Pianos in the Shrine to Music Museum." M.M. thesis, University of South Dakota, 1991.

Arranged chronologically by type of piano (grand pianos, *Tangentenflügel*, harp piano, square pianos, upright pianos). Each entry includes the catalog number and may include information about the builder, date, location, signatures and/or other inscriptions, compass, pedals, acquisition history, measurements, constructional details, action, dampers, keyboard, stringing and scaling, the current condition, as well as a list of other instruments by the builder, relevant background information, a selective bibliography, illustrations, and photographs. A more comprehensive bibliography at the end of the document. 160 pp.

724. Koster, John. *Keyboard Musical Instruments in the Museum of Fine Arts, Boston.* Boston: Museum of Fine Arts, 1994.

With contributions by Sheridan Germann and John T. Kirk. Illustrated by Stephen Korbet and the author. Detailed descriptions with measurements of the fifty-four historical keyboard instruments at the Boston Museum of Fine Arts. Includes six grand pianos, thirteen square pianos, three upright pianos, two other pianos, and a Steinert piano action. Appendix A: a list of modern instruments of historical type at the museum, with brief descriptions;

appendix B: a glossary of wood terminology; appendix C: a general glossary. Photographs, illustrations, tables. Bibliography. 368 pp.

725. Kottick, Edward L., and George Lucktenberg. *Early Keyboard Instruments in European Museums*. Bloomington: Indiana University Press, 1997.

A list of the European museums with early keyboard instruments, organized by country. Includes addresses, hours, phone and fax numbers of the museums. Background information and descriptions of the instruments housed by each museum. Includes harpsichords, clavichords, and pianos. Photographs. Glossary. 276 pp.

726. Libin, Laurence [Elliot]. *American Musical Instruments in the Metropolitan Museum of Art*. With a foreword by Philippe de Montebello and a preface by Henry Steinway. New York: Metropolitan Museum of Art; New York: W. W. Norton & Company, 1985.

Backgrounds and descriptions of the American musical instruments housed in the museum. Includes a chapter on keyboard and automata. Photographs, illustrations. Bibliography. 224 pp.

————. *Keynotes: Two Centuries of Piano Design. See 105 under* History—General History.

727. Longaker, Mark. "Time Machines: Part III, Private Collections." *Early Music America* 4, no. 4 (Winter 1998–1999): 23–28.

Features some private collections of early instruments, including Edmund Frederick's piano collection. A selected discography of recordings on the instruments in the featured collections. Photographs.

728. Mactaggart, Peter, and Ann Mactaggart, eds. *Musical Instruments in the 1851 Exhibition: A Transcription of the Entries of Musical Interest from the Official Illustrated Catalogue of the Great Exhibition of the Art and Industry of All Nations, with Additional Ma-*

*terial from Contemporary Sources*. Welwyn, England: Mac & Me, 1986.

Alphabetical listings of instruments by manufacturer, patentee/inventor, or proprietor, classified by instrument types. Includes a section devoted to pianos (pp. 15–44). An entry may include location of the manufacturer, names and locations of agents, description of the instrument, and other relevant information, and may be annotated. Includes reports of the jury and a list of the awards at the exhibition. Illustrations. Bibliography. 109 pp.

729. Metropolitan Museum of Art. *The Crosby Brown Collection of Musical Instruments of All Nations: Catalogue of Keyboard Instruments*. With an introduction by A. J. Hipkins. New York: Metropolitan Museum of Art, 1903.

Photographs, illustrations, and descriptions of the keyboard instruments in the collection. Includes plucked stringed keyboard instruments (such as the psaltery, spinet, harpsichord, and clavicytherium), struck stringed keyboard instruments (such as the dulcimer, clavichord, and piano), bowed stringed keyboard instruments, keyboard wind instruments (such as the organ), keyboard instruments with other sounding mechanisms, and accessories. An entry may include information about the compass, dimensions, case and appearance, pedals, inscriptions and nameboards, stringing, other constructional features, and other background information. Appendices contain illustrations and descriptions of various actions and action parts and translations of documents related to the first Cristofori piano. 313 pp.

730. Michel, N[orman] E[lwood]. *"Historical Pianos": Harpsichords and Clavichords*. Pico Rivera, Calif.: by the author, 1970.

A photographic collection of pianos. Photographs of pianos, birthplaces, family homes, museums, and historical societies of thirty-seven presidents of the United States from Washington to Nixon, pp. 1–48. Photographs of pianos, clavichords, harpsichords, and homes of statesmen, actors, actresses, royalty, writers, and other notable persons, pp. 49–76. Photographs from libraries, historical societies, museums, and other institutions, pp. 77–135.

Photographs of musical instruments from all over the world, pp. 136–236. 236 pp.

731. ———. *Old Pianos*. Rivera, Calif.: by the author, 1954.

A collection of black-and-white photographs of instruments with descriptions and relevant information (such as builder/manufacturer, serial number, current location, and dates where known). Includes spinets, clavichords, harpsichords, squares, and other musical instruments. 181 pp.

732. The National Trust of Australia (N. S. W.) Women's Committee, comp. *Antiques Australia: First Fleet to Federation*. Sydney: National Trust of Australia, 1976.

Compiled in association with the Museum of Applied Arts & Sciences, Sydney. Photographs by Charles Turner and J. S. Whitelock. A catalog for the Antiques Australia exhibition at Lindesay in 1976, which included the oldest surviving Australian-made piano. 23 pp.

733. Patey, Carol. *Musical Instruments at the Victoria & Albert Museum: An Introduction*. London: Her Majesty's Stationery Office, 1978.

A catalog of the historical instruments at the museum. Photographs and brief descriptions of the instruments, including a 1810 giraffe piano. Bibliography. 31 pp.

734. Pressley, Nancy Gamble. "Winterthur Museum's Early American Keyboard and Music Collections: An Example of Museum Resources for Music in Higher Education." Ph.D. dissertation, Southern Illinois University at Carbondale, 1982.

A study of the keyboard instruments, keyboard music, and bibliographical materials at the museum (located near Wilmington, Del.). Examines each instrument in detail, noting physical description, the historical context of the instrument and the musical life behind the instrument, restoration details, and other relevant facts, with photograph of each instrument. Background information about the museum. Bibliography. 113 pp.

735. Rogan, John P. *Antiques in Australia from Private Collections.* With a foreword by Joseph Burke. Brisbane, Australia: Jacaranda, 1975.

A photographic collection of antiques in private homes in Australia. The photographs are accompanied by general descriptions and some background information. Includes a grand piano by Broadwood (1801) and a cabinet piano by Clementi (1815). Photographs by John H. Gumley. 244 pp.

736. Schott, Howard. *Keyboard Instruments.* Victoria and Albert Museum Catalogue of Musical Instruments, ed. Peter Thorton, vol. 1. 2nd ed. London: Her Majesty's Stationery Office, 1985.

Lists historical harpsichords, clavichords, and pianos, by date. Each entry may contain a photograph of the instrument, physical description, and information about the origin of the instrument, dates, and inscription, as well as other background information. Bibliography. 94 pp., plus 59 pp. of plates.

737. Smithsonian Institution. *A Checklist of Keyboard Instruments at the Smithsonian Institution.* Washington, D.C.: Smithsonian Institution, 1967.

A list of the keyboard instruments at the institution with brief descriptions of each instrument (such as builder, catalog number, place of origin, date, type, compass, and pedals). Includes pianos, harpsichords, clavichords, organs, and other miscellaneous keyboard instruments. Glossary. Photographs of some of the instruments. 79 pp.

738. Stanley, Albert A. *Catalogue of the Stearns Collection of Musical Instruments.* 2nd ed. Ann Arbor: University of Michigan, 1921.

Contains descriptions (appearance, dimensions, signature) of the historical instruments in the collection including several pianos (see class V, section C). Some entries contain additional background information. Bibliography. 276 pp., plus plates.

Winternitz, Emanuel. *Keyboard Instruments in the Metropolitan*

*Museum of Art: A Picture Book. See 153 under* History—General
History.

## Pedal Piano

739. Ford, Karrin Elizabeth. "The *Pedalklavier*: Its Influence on the
Keyboard Works of Schumann and Other Nineteenth-Century
Composers." D.M.A. thesis, University of Cincinnati, 1984.

A history of the stringed keyboard instruments with pedalboards. Discusses the pedal clavichord, the pedal harpsichord, and
the pedal piano; also discusses the pedal harmonium briefly. Topics include construction, builders, and literature. Appendix A:
translated excerpts about the pedal clavichord or pedal harpsichord from the eighteenth and nineteenth centuries. Appendix B: a
chronological list of surviving pedal clavichords, harpsichords,
and pianos, with their dates, places of origin, names of builders,
and present locations of the instruments. Appendix C: illustrations.
Appendix D: a list of advertisements for pedal pianos and pedal
attachments, with sources and dates. Bibliography, discography,
and a list of works for the instruments. 197 pp.

740. ————. "The Pedal Piano." *Journal of Church Music* 27, no. 4
(April 1985): 17–18.

An overview of string keyboard instruments with pedalboards,
primarily from the standpoint of organists. Photograph.

741. ————. "The Pedal Piano." *Diapason* 75, no. 10 (October 1984):
10–11; no. 11 (November 1984): 6; no. 12 (December 1984):
14–15.

Discusses the history of the pedal piano. Topics include
construction, builders, literature, and the place of the instrument in
the musical society. Photographs.

742. ————. "The Pedal Piano: A Forgotten Instrument." *American
Music Teacher* 35, no. 2 (November–December 1985): 43–45.

An introductory article about the instrument. Addresses

history, construction, and literature. Photographs, illustrations.

743. ———. "The Pedal Piano in America 1875–1900." *American Organist* 18, no. 10 (October 1984): 43–45.

Compares the history of the instrument in America to that in Europe, and discusses pedal piano makers in America. Illustrations.

744. Jones, N. Holford. "An Electrically-Operated Pedalboard." *Organ* 52, no. 207 (1973): 123–36.

Step-by-step instructions on how to build an electrical pedalboard and attach it to a piano to make a pedal piano. A list of necessary items at the end. Illustrations (many labeled).

745. Maunder, Richard, and David Rowland. "Instruments: Mozart's Pedal Piano." *Early Music* 23, no. 2 (May 1995): 287–96.

Discusses Mozart's relationship with the instrument by examining documents and his works. Addresses construction of his pedal piano, repertory, and performance implications of the study. Photograph, illustrations.

746. Sadie, Stanley, ed. *The New Grove Dictionary of Music and Musicians*. 20 vols. London: Macmillan, 1980. S.v. "Pedal Pianoforte," by Edwin M. Ripin.

A brief article about the history of the pedal piano. Photograph on p. 329.

747. Wells, John. "Charles Valentin Alkan (1813–1888): Parts III & IV." *Organists' Review* 75, no. 2 (May 1989): 107–11.

Includes an appendix that summarizes the history of the pedal piano and Alkan's relationship with the instrument.

## Composers and the Piano

### General

748. Bianchi, Michael. "A Piano with a Past." *Clavier* 19, no. 1 (January 1980): 53.

An essay about a Bechstein piano known to have been played by Liszt, Anton Rubinstein, Brahms, Bartók, Dohnanyi, Kodaly, among others.

Golightly, John Wesley. "The Piano between 1800 and 1850: The Instruments for Which the Composers Wrote." *See 75 under* History—General History.

### Beethoven

749. Curtis, David. "Beethoven's Piano." *Clavier* 15, no. 1 (January 1976): 17–18.

An essay about the circumstances surrounding Beethoven's acquisition of his Broadwood piano. Photograph, illustration.

Drake, Kenneth. "Behind the Fallboard." *See 263 under* Builders and Manufacturers—Broadwood.

750. Fontana, Eszter. "Beethoven's London Piano and the Viennese Piano Makers." *New Hungarian Quarterly* 33, no. 125 (Spring 1992): 153–55.

Discusses Beethoven's acquisition of the Broadwood piano and his request for its restoration.

Ludden, Bennet. "Beethoven's Broadwood: A Present-Day Memoir." *See 265 under* Builders and Manufacturers—Broadwood.

Melville, Derek. "Beethoven's Pianos." *See 266 under* Builders and Manufacturers—Broadwood.

751. Newman, William S. "Beethoven's Pianos versus His Piano Ideals." *Journal of the American Musicological Society* 23, no. 3 (Fall 1970): 484–504.

A comparison of Beethoven's pianos (through his three surviving pianos) to his piano ideals as reflected in his piano works. Discusses compass, pedals, actions, and tone. Bibliography.

Sumner, William L[eslie]. "Beethoven and the Pianoforte." *See 174 under* History—Austria and Germany.

Wythe, Deborah. "The Pianos of Conrad Graf." *See 314 under* Builders and Manufacturers—Graf, Conrad

Winston, David. "Other Voices, Other Rooms: An Instrument Tells Its Own Story." *See 666 under* Maintenance and Repair—Rebuilding and Restoration.

———. "The Restoration of Beethoven's 1817 Broadwood Grand Piano." *See 667 under* Maintenance and Repair—Rebuilding and Restoration.

## Brahms

752. Bozarth, George Z., and Stephen H. Brady. "The Pianos of Johannes Brahms." In *Brahms and His World*, ed. Walter Frisch, 49–64. Princeton: Princeton University Press, 1990.

Discusses pianos owned and/or played by Brahms, including the 1839 Graf and the 1868 Streicher pianos. Photographs.

Wythe, Deborah. "The Pianos of Conrad Graf." *See 314 under* Builders and Manufacturers—Graf, Conrad

## Chopin

Ripoll, Luis. *Chopin's Pianos: The Pleyel in Majorca. See 338 under*

Builders and Manufacturers—Pleyel.

## Haydn

Gates, Robert Edward. "The Influence of the Eighteenth-Century Piano on the Music of Joseph Haydn." *See 69 under* History—General History.

Hollis, Helen Rice. *The Musical Instruments of Joseph Haydn: An Introduction. See 93 under* History—General History.

## Liszt

Keeling, Geraldine. "Liszt and J. B. Streicher, a Viennese Piano Maker." *See 384 under* Builders and Manufacturers—Streicher.

753. ———. "The Liszt Pianos—Some Aspects of Preference and Technology." *New Hungarian Quarterly* 27, no. 104 (Winter 1986): 220–32.

Addresses pianos associated with Liszt and their construction. Discusses compass, action, frame, stringing, pedals, and pianos with multiple keyboards.

Stevenson, Robert. "Liszt in Andalusia." *See 254 under* Builders and Manufacturers—Boisselot.

## Mendelssohn

754. Parkins, Robert. "Mendelssohn and the Erard Piano." *Piano Quarterly* 32, no. 125 (Spring 1984): 53–58.

Discusses Mendelssohn's encounter with various pianos, particularly his Erard piano. Inferences about the instrument are made through examining an Erard grand (from around the same time) in the collection of the Metropolitan Museum of Art, New York.

# Mozart

755. Badura-Skoda, Eva. "Mozart's Piano." *American Music Teacher* 12, no. 6 (July–August 1963): 12–13.

An essay about pianos owned by Mozart. Also mentions Haydn's pianos. Photograph.

Latcham, Michael. "Mozart and the Pianos of Gabriel Anton Walter." *See 388 under* Builders and Manufacturers—Walter.

756. Maunder, Richard. "Mozart's Keyboard Instruments." *Early Music* 20, no. 2 (May 1992): 207–19.

Discusses the harpsichords, clavichords, and fortepianos owned or played by Mozart. Photographs.

Maunder, Richard, and David Rowland. "Instruments: Mozart's Pedal Piano." *See 745 under* Miscellaneous—Pedal Piano.

# Scarlatti

757. Sutherland, David. "Domenico Scarlatti and the Florentine Piano." *Early Music* 23, no. 2 (May 1995): 243–56.

Discusses possible influences of the Florentine piano on Scarlatti. Photograph.

758. van der Meer, John Henry. "The Keyboard Instruments at the Disposal of Domenico Scarlatti." *Galpin Society Journal* no. 50 (March 1997): 136–60.

Compares compasses of the instruments accessible to Scarlatti to the ranges of his works. Considers dates and Scarlatti's location at the time.

# Schumann

Wythe, Deborah. "The Pianos of Conrad Graf." *See 314 under* Builders and Manufacturers—Graf, Conrad

# Selection and Purchase

759. Amrein, Edward J. "Specifications for School Pianos." *Music Journal* 15, no. 1 (January 1957): 27–28, 49.

Offers tips in selecting pianos for institutional use, particularly for schools. Discusses parts of the piano and sound.

760. Bull, Robert P. "Want a Piano? Take Your Time!" *Music Journal* 28, no. 2 (February 1970): 30–31.

Discusses considerations in purchasing a piano, primarily for parents with children who are beginners. Photographs.

761. *Buyer's Guide for Professional-Quality Pianos.* [South Haven, Mich.: Everett Piano Company, 1976].

Discusses types and styles of pianos, sizes, new versus used pianos, dealers and brand names, construction, tone, and other purchase considerations. Some special considerations for school pianos are treated in a separate section at the end. Photographs (some labeled), illustrations. Glossary. 29 pp.

762. "Buying a Piano." *Music Teacher and Piano Student* 45, no. 1 (January 1966): 13–14; no. 2 (February 1966): 65, 78; no. 3 (March 1966): 122; no. 4 (April 1966): 165.

This series of articles compiles selection criteria for a piano by performers, music school administrators, and teachers. Includes comments from an expert in music instrument technology.

763. "Buying a Used Piano." *Clavier* 34, no. 1 (January 1995): 36.

Primarily intended for parents of beginning students.

764. "Condition and Care of the Pupil's Piano." *Music Teacher and Piano Student* 38, no. 2 (February 1959): 73, 89.

Discusses selection and purchase of the piano. Discusses

reconditioned pianos and after-services as well as general tips for selection.

765. Doerschuk, Robert L. "How to Buy a Piano." *Keyboard* 19, no. 12 (December 1993): 104, 105, 107.

Addresses the motivation for purchasing, sound, strings, hammers, action, pedals, keys, materials, special considerations for vertical pianos, and warranty and delivery services.

766. Esterowitz, Michael. "Piano Doctor: How to Buy a Used Piano, Part I." *Keyboard Classics* 4, no. 6 (November–December 1984): 45.

Discusses cost, style, exterior case, and tuning. Continued in "Piano Doctor: How to Check a Used Piano." *Keyboard Classics* 5, no. 1 (January–February 1985): 47; no. 2 (March–April 1985): 42; no. 3 (May–June 1985): 40, by the same author.

767. ———. "Piano Doctor: How to Check a Used Piano." *Keyboard Classics* 5, no. 1 (January–February 1985): 47; no. 2 (March–April 1985): 42; no. 3 (May–June 1985): 40.

Continued from "Piano Doctor: How to Buy a Used Piano, Part I," *Keyboard Classics* 4, no. 6 (November–December 1984): 45, by the same author. Discusses checking the bridge, strings, keyboard, action, hammers, and dampers.

Fine, Larry. *The Piano Book: Buying & Owning a New or Used Piano. See 408 under* Construction and Design—General Construction.

768. ———. "The Piano Technician: Feeling at Home with Your New Piano." *Keyboard* 12, no. 8 (August 1986): 118.

Discusses working with a dealer and a technician after the purchase and some precautions before purchase.

769. ———. "The Piano Technician: Looking at Legs and Lids." *Keyboard* 11, no. 6 (June 1985): 78.

Discusses piano cabinetry when purchasing a piano. Addresses legs and casters, style and finish, fallboard, lid, music rack, key-bed, and serviceability.

———. "The Piano Technician: Piano Hammers: Another Favorite Site for Sales Gimmicks." *See 498 under* Construction and Design—Hammers.

770. ———. "The Piano Technician: Stalking the 'Reputable' Piano Dealer." *Keyboard* 12, no. 5 (May 1986): 96.

Discusses how to select a dealer from whom to purchase a piano.

771. Gatz, P. W. "You and Your Piano: Buying a New Piano." *Music Journal* 11, no. 4 (April 1953): 30–31.

Discusses the action, upright versus grand pianos, cost, style, and choosing a dealer.

772. ———. "You and Your Piano: Buying a Used Piano." *Music Journal* 11, no. 5 (May 1953): 34–38; no. 6 (June 1953): 36, 38.

Discusses the age of the piano, cast-iron plate, soundboard, bridges, tuning pins and pinblock, strings, keys, action, dampers, and pedals. Also addresses purchasing a player piano.

Goff, Hardy N. *Goff's Money Saving Piano Guide. See 534 under* Maintenance and Repair—General Maintenance and Repair.

773. Gould, Brian. *Buying a Square Piano.* Bedford Park, England: Naples Press, 1968.

Discusses considerations in selecting a square piano for purchase. Includes background information about square pianos. 6 pp., unpaginated.

774. Harris, Brian. "Keyboards: Buying a Piano." *Canadian Musician* 4, no. 4 (July–August 1982): 81.

Discusses grand versus upright pianos, size, cost, new versus used pianos, the condition, and brands.

Hasluck, Paul N[ooncree]. *Pianos: Their Construction, Tuning, and Repair, with Numerous Engravings and Diagrams. See 413 under* Construction and Design—General Construction.

Hobbs, H[enry]. *The Piano in India: How to Keep It in Order: Practical Information on Repairing, Regulating, Tuning, Packing, and Treatment of Pianofortes in Tropical Climates. See 537 under* Maintenance and Repair—General Maintenance and Repair.

775. Hodsdon, Alec. "On Buying a Square Piano." *Musical Times and Singing Class Circular* 91 (February 1950): 67.

   Addresses selecting a square piano for purchase, with special consideration for repair possibilities. Discusses checking for wear, damages in the case and the legs, and other internal damages.

Hoskins, Leslie J. "Do All Pianos Sound Alike? Some Background Information to Review before Shopping for That New Piano." *See 414 under* Construction and Design—General Construction.

Johannesen, Grant. "Ups and Downs of Piano Action." *See 477 under* Construction and Design—Action.

776. Kahler, Claire Eugene. "A Practical Guide to Aid in the Purchase of a New or Used Piano for Use in the Home, Church or School." M.M. thesis, Kansas State University, 1973.

   Topics include the construction of the modern piano, considerations for purchasing a new or used piano, and some issues in basic maintenance and care. Discusses the potential player, the size and type, volume, action, pedals, style and finish, cost, warranty, condition (if used), and brand names. Bibliography, glossary. 39 pp.

777. Leverett, Willard M. *How to Buy a Good Used Piano.* Arvada, Colo.: by the author, 1978. Reprint, Arvada, Colo.: by the author, 1988.

   A photographic guide on selecting and purchasing a used piano. Discusses how to evaluate the piano (including how to remove panels and the fallboard on uprights), which parts of the piano to examine, considerations for purchasing, general maintenance and care, and moving. Addresses consoles, studio pianos (for schools, churches, and home), spinets, and grand pianos. Also includes general information about player pianos. 69 pp.

778. Mangialetti, Nada. "How to Buy a Piano." *Music Journal* 33, no. 6 (July 1975): 10–12, 61–62. Reprint, *Journal of Church Music* 19, no. 7 (September 1977): 11–15.

Discusses brand, size, new versus used pianos, touch, and sound. Includes a checklist for evaluating used pianos, and tips for basic maintenance of the piano.

779. Marceaux, Verne R. "The Piano Tragedy." *School Musician* 26, no. 9 (May 1955): 16–17.

Discusses the problems in purchasing pianos for schools and other considerations.

780. McCalley, Grace. "Many Choices in Buying a Piano." *Clavier* 36, no. 8 (October 1997): 42–44.

Discusses cost and evaluating piano quality.

Miller, Harold. *The Rise and Decline of the Piano: Care and Use of the Piano. See 422 under* Construction and Design—General Construction.

781. Mohn, Norman Carroll. "Wanted: A Good Used Piano." *Piano Teacher* 7, no. 3 (January–February 1965): 14–15.

Discusses the action, hammers, tuning pins, bridle straps, soundboard, pedals, and tone.

782. Montparker, Carol. "Buying a New Piano? Consult an Expert." *Clavier* 20, no. 10 (December 1981): 46–47.

An interview with piano technician Franz Mohr on selecting a new piano for purchase. Discusses sound, soundboard, touch, key covering, and action.

783. ———. "Buying a Used Piano? Consult an Expert." *Clavier* 21, no. 1 (January 1982): 54–55.

An interview with piano technician Franz Mohr on selecting a used piano for purchase. Discusses condition of the piano, action, soundboard, pedals, pinblock, finish, grand versus vertical pianos, and old versus new pianos.

"Music Trade Forum: Grand or Upright?" *See 423 under* Construction and Design—General Construction.

784. "The New Piano." *Music Teacher and Piano Student* 46, no. 5 (May 1967): 11–12.

Discusses considerations in selecting a piano for purchase. Addresses materials and technology, new versus used pianos, the condition, brand names and dealers, and other issues concerning the construction of the piano.

785. Olejarz, Walter, Jr. *Modern Piano Buyers Guide*. Bristol, Conn.: by the author, 1980.

A booklet primarily addressing selection and purchase of a piano. Topics include history of the instrument, types and styles of pianos, prices of pianos and repairs (selective information, current as of the time of publication), moving, refinishing, and playing. Includes a glossary, a list of miscellaneous facts, and a business directory of instructors, dealers, and technicians in Connecticut (at the time of publication). 58 pp.

786. Pantoga, Fritzie. "Pianos for Sale." *Clavier* 19, no. 7 (September 1980): 56–57.

Adapted from "Buy Lines," *Evanston Review*, February 1, 1979, pp. 106–8. Tips on buying used pianos, rebuilt pianos, and new pianos, with cost considerations. Includes "Guidelines in Shopping for a New Piano."

787. "Pianos: Fine Tune Your Choices." *Changing Times* 40, no. 1 (January 1986): 70–74.

Discusses considerations in selecting and purchasing a piano. Discusses price, piano parts and their qualities, and new versus used pianos. Includes tips on basic care and maintenance of the instrument.

788. Pond, Gregory. *The Piano Handbook: A Guide to Buying, Maintaining, and Selling Your Piano.* N.p.: Curtis Enterprises, 1980.

The primary focus is on selecting and purchasing. Topics include brands and models, construction, structural condition of the piano, sound, and cost. Includes a short section on basic maintenance and care at the end. Photographs, illustrations (labeled). 50 pp.

789. Porter, Thomas. "So You're Going to Buy a Piano." *Clavier* 11, no. 5 (May–June 1972): 14–16.

Discusses some considerations in purchasing a piano. Addresses new, used, and rebuilt pianos.

"The Problem with Bad Pianos." *See 553 under* Maintenance and Repair—General Maintenance and Repair.

Rawlings, Kim. *The Best Piano Buyer's Guide. See 432 under* Construction and Design—General Construction.

790. Reid, Graham. "Tips for Buying a Piano." *Piano Quarterly* 35, no. 137 (Spring 1987): 45.

Discusses appraisals, size, and upright versus grand pianos.

791. Roope, W. "Hints on Purchasing a Reconditioned Piano." *Music Teacher and Piano Student* 31, no. 5 (March 1952): 238.

Discusses brand names, sound, tuning, strings, action, keys, and appearance.

792. Roseman, Ellen. "Quality Key to Piano Buying." *Ragtimer* (September–October 1980): 12–13.

Originally published in *Toronto Globe and Mail.* Discusses, costs, size, and other physical features. Addresses new, used, and rebuilt pianos, as well as rentals.

Schmeckel, Carl D. *The Piano Owner's Guide: How to Buy and Care for a Piano. See 438 under* Construction and Design—General Construction.

793. Shapiro, Bob. *The Book on Pianos: Or Everything (Almost) You Wanted to Know about Pianos but Didn't Know Who to Ask.* Atlanta: IRS Systems, 1997.

General guidelines on selecting and purchasing a piano. Topics include construction, styles and types of pianos, brands, renting versus purchasing, dealers, and price. Illustrations. 19 pp.

794. "Some Practical Hints on Selecting and Choosing a Piano." *Music Teacher and Piano Student* 31, no. 11 (November 1952): 535.

Discusses grand versus upright pianos, tone quality, touch, and appearance. Includes a brief discussion of the grand action.

795. Sullivan, Alfred D. "The Crusading Piano Tuner: A Plea to Manufacturers, a Warning to Purchasers to Check Quality." *Clavier* 14, no. 5 (May–June 1975): 31–35.

An article about the author's experiences and problems in selecting pianos for his clients. Focus on American pianos.

796. Tasciotti, Lou. "Selecting a Rebuilt Piano." *Clavier* 35, no. 2 (February 1996): 18–19.

Discusses the cost, sound, finish, soundboard, bridges, strings and tuning pins, key covering, and the action.

797. Thorne, Carol. "Problems with Used Pianos." *Clavier* 36, no. 10 (December 1997): 26.

Addresses issues in purchasing used pianos with the intent to rebuild. From discussions by Mark Foss, a piano rebuilder in the Chicago area.

798. Waite, Roy E. "How to Buy a Piano." *House Beautiful* 93, no. 8 (August 1951): 48–49, 121.

About selecting a piano for purchase as a piece of furniture as well as a musical instrument. Photographs.

West, Richard E. *Notes on the Piano: Questions and Answers about Piano Care and Piano Buying. See 569 under* Maintenance and Repair—General Maintenance and Repair.

799. Wiens, Mary. "Guide to Finding a Vintage Upright." *Music Magazine* 8, no. 2 (March–April 1985): 20–22.

Discusses purchasing used pianos, with some special considerations for buying older pianos for restoration. Photograph, illustration.

800. Williams, Loren R. "Making and Protecting—An Investment." *Church Musician* 14, no. 3 (March 1963): 12–14.

Discusses basic maintenance and selecting the piano for church use.

Wood, Lawrence R[obert]. *Pianos, Anyone? See 575 under* Maintenance and Repair—General Maintenance and Repair.

Woodman, H. Staunton. *How to Tune a Piano, How to Clean Your Piano and Keep It in Good Condition, How to Buy a Used Piano. See 576 under* Maintenance and Repair—General Maintenance and Repair.

801. Zolper, Stephen. "Tips on Purchasing Used Pianos." *Clavier* 34, no. 10 (December 1995): 33–34.

Discusses purchasing used or rebuilt pianos. Addresses appearance, sound, soundboard, pinblock, hammers, dampers, strings, and pedals.

## Juvenile

802. Anderson, David. *The Piano Makers*. New York: Pantheon Books, 1982.

A step-by-step photographic introduction to piano making, primarily for children. Includes a section about how the piano action works, with labeled photographs of the action. 55 pp.

803. Blocksma, Mary. *The Marvelous Music Machine: A Story of the Piano*. Englewood Cliffs, N.J.: Prentice-Hall, 1984.

Illustrated by Mischa Richter. Intended for children. Discusses general information and miscellaneous trivia, history, construction, playing, and basic maintenance of the piano. 58 pp., unpaginated.

Burton, Ken. *"Dear Dr. Piano . . . ": Piano Facts and Fun. See 5 under* General.

804. Davis, Lionel, and Edith Davis. *Keyboard Instruments: The Story of the Piano*. Minneapolis: Lerner Publications Company, 1963.

Prepared under the supervision of Robert W. Surplus. A general information book about the instrument. Topics include performance, composition, and construction. Intended for children. 41 pp.

Guy, Suzanne [W.], and Donna [M.] Lacy. *The Music Box: The Story of Cristofori. See 288 under* Builders and Manufacturers—Cristofori.

805. Howard, Roy E. "How to Keep Your Upright Sounding Grand." *Music Educators Journal* 72, no. 3 (November 1985): 52–56.

An introduction to piano construction, primarily for school children on school instruments. Discusses the cabinet, the action, sound, basic structure of the piano, and tuning. Includes tips on moving the piano, diagnosing common problems, and evaluating an older piano.

806. Isherwood, Millicent. *The Piano*. Oxford Topics in Music, ed. Kenneth and Valerie McLeish. Oxford: Oxford University Press, 1981.

   An illustrated/photographic introduction to the piano, intended for eleven to fourteen-year-olds. Addresses history, construction, manufacturers, pedagogues and pedagogy, composers and literature, performing, performers, and genres. Each chapter is concluded with questions and projects. 48 pp.

807. Lewis, Patricia Ann. "A Unit of Piano Design for Use in Junior High School General Music Classes." M.M. thesis, Pittsburg State University, 1980.

   A set of lesson plans for a music appreciation class at the junior high school level. Topics include construction, acoustics, history, and basic maintenance and care. Reviews and tests. Illustrations (labeled). Bibliography. 39 pp.

808. Turner, Barrie Carson. *The Living Piano*. New York: Alfred A. Knopf, 1996.

   An illustrated/photographic introduction to the piano. Discusses history, construction, literature, composers, performance, and performers. Accompanied by a CD. Primarily for younger readers. 48 pp.

# Other Miscellaneous Topics

809. Campbell, Denele Pitts. *Notes of a Piano Tuner*. Sarasota, Fla.: Pineapple Press, 1997.

   An essay about the author's experiences (not necessarily related to piano technology) as a piano tuner. 141 pp.

810. Carmi, Avner, and Hannah Carmi. *The Immortal Piano*. New York: Crown Publishers, 1960.

   An account of an Israeli piano technician's quest for a legendary piano and the restoration of the instrument. 288 pp.

811. Darreg, Ivor. *Shall We Improve the Piano?* Los Angeles: by the author, [1965].

> An essay about various attempts to improve the piano, and the author's proposal for an equal temperament keyboard with more than twelve tones to an octave. Includes a selective bibliography and a partial list of compositions for the piano by the author. Illustrations. 31 pp.

812. "The Doig Transposing Piano." *Musical Opinion and Music Trade Review* 76, no. 909 (June 1953): 524.

> A short report about the instrument. Discusses its features in construction and mechanics.

813. Fischer, Bernard. "The Pianos, Organs, and Other Musical Instruments and Materials' Industry with Special Reference to Its Location." M.A. thesis, University of Chicago, 1929.

> Discusses the distribution of the piano industry in the United States, with a focus on the Chicago area. Illustrations. Bibliography. 140 pp.

814. "International Trade Commission to Investigate Piano Industry." *Music Trades* 147, no. 1 (February 1999): 61.

> A short report about the investigation into whether Asian piano manufacturers are "dumping" pianos in the U.S. Comments on prior investigations into the music industry by the commission.

815. Milano, Dominic. "Keyboard Report: Helpinstill Roadmaster." *Keyboard* 7, no. 9 (September 1981): 64.

> A short report on Helpinstill Roadmaster, a portable acoustic piano. Discusses keyboard, controls, soundboard, portability, and tuning. Photograph.

816. "Music Trade Forum: A Social Problem." *Musical Opinion* 87, no. 1035 (December 1963): 189.

> Discusses ways to muffle piano sounds, particularly those of a grand piano.

Neupert, W. D. "Investigation of the Structure-Borne Sound of Pianos in Homes." *See 464 under* Construction and Design—Acoustics.

817. Rice, Emert S. "One Small Voice (1980)." TMs (Photocopy). South Caroliniana Forum Club Collection, University of South Carolina, Columbia, S.C.

The document chronicles the author's experience in challenging the federal government on issues that concerned him. The second part of this two-part document discusses the excise tax imposed on reconditioned pianos after World War II. As background material the pre- and postwar states of the piano trade are briefly explained. Apparently the author of the paper owned a shop that reconditioned old pianos (uprights and grands) in Columbia, S.C. Includes a two-page illustrated attachment titled "The Procedure for 'Cutting Down' an Upright Piano." 21 leaves, partially paginated.

818. Ross, Nancy L. "Imports Spark Piano Revival." *Washington Post*, 2 February 1987, Washington Business section, pp. 1, 28–30.

Discusses the effects of imported pianos on the piano market in the United States. Photographs, illustrations.

819. Slonimsky, Nicholas. "Musical Miscellany." *Etude* 68 (February 1950): 4–5.

Includes a brief description and a photograph of an eight-octave piano located in Paris and an anecdote about Thomas Jefferson and his piano purchase.

820. "Steingraeber & Söhne: Pianos for the Handicapped." *Musik international—Instrumentenbau-Zeitschrift* 39, no. 12 (December 1985): 779–80.

A short report on an attachment that replaces the damper pedals for handicapped players.

821. "Tough Pianos." *Musical Times and Singing-Class Circular* 92, no. 1303 (September 1951): 422.

A short report on abuse- and damage-resistant pianos designed by Robert Clarke and made by Alfred Knight (of Edmonton) and Major A. Wheatley (of Lambert's in London).

822. "U.S. Investigates Unfair Foreign Piano Competition: U.S. Trade Commission Explores Whether China and Indonesia Are Dumping Cheap Uprights in the U.S. Market." *Music Trades* 147, no. 3 (April 1999): 66, 69–70, 72, 74, 77.

A report on the hearing before the International Trade Commission on February 17, 1999, in Washington, D.C. Representatives from Baldwin, Story & Clark, Kawai, and Samick gave testimonies in the investigation started by Baldwin's complaint to the House Ways and Means Committee. Photographs.

# Subject Index

# Author Index

*Note: The numbers following an author's name refer to the entry numbers rather than page numbers.*

# Title Index

*Note: The numbers following a title refer to the entry numbers rather than page numbers.*

# About the Author

Michiko Ishiyama Wolcott, a native of Japan, received her early music training in her home country. Since her arrival in the United States at the age of fifteen, she has studied piano with Sally Northcutt, Ann Schein, Marilyn Neeley, Enid Katahn, and James Streem. She received a bachelor of music degree in piano performance from Florida State University in 1990, a master of music degree in piano performance from the Peabody Conservatory in 1992, a master of music degree in music theory from Florida State University in 1996, and a doctor of music degree in piano performance from Florida State University in 2000. Winner of many awards and honors, including the prestigious Presser Scholarship, she has performed with the Alabama Symphony Orchestra and the Florida State University Symphony, while performing extensively in the eastern United States as a soloist and a chamber musician. In addition, she has a master of science degree in statistics from Florida State University, taught piano, music theory, and statistics as a teaching assistant, and won honors as a statistics student. Currently, she is a statistical analyst in Atlanta, Georgia.